Get more
– and more value –
from your people

Alan Fowler has worked widely in both the private and public sectors, with personnel appointments in four industries and two local authorities. He is now a freelance consultant, a director of Personnel Publications Ltd, and a member of the editorial board of *People Management*, the fortnightly journal of the IPD. He writes extensively on personnel issues, with regular articles in *People Management* and the *Local Government Chronicle*. His books include *The Disciplinary Interview* (1996) and *Negotiating, Persuading and Influencing* (1995), both in the IPD's Management Shapers series; *Negotiation Skills and Strategies* (second edition 1996); *Redundancy* (1993); *Taking Charge: A guide to people management in today's public sector* (1993); and a companion volume to the present one, *Get More – and More Results – from Your People* (1998). All these titles are published by the IPD.

The Institute of Personnel and Development is the leading publisher of books and reports for personnel and training professionals, students, and all those concerned with the effective management and development of people at work. For details of all our titles, please contact the Publishing Department:

tel. 0181-263 3387

fax. 0181-263 3850

e-mail publish@ipd.co.uk

The catalogue of all IPD titles can be viewed on the IPD website:

http://www.ipd.co.uk

Get more
– *and more value* –
from your people

Alan Fowler

INSTITUTE OF PERSONNEL AND DEVELOPMENT

First published in 1998

Typesetting by Wyvern 21, Bristol
and printed in Great Britain by
the Cromwell Press, Trowbridge, Wiltshire

British Library Cataloguing in Publication Data
A catalogue record for this book is available from the British Library

ISBN 0-85292-747-9

The views expressed in this book are the author's own and may not necessarily reflect those of the IPD.

IPD House, Camp Road, Wimbledon, London SW19 4UX
Tel: 0181-971-9000   Fax: 0181-263-3333
Registered office as above. Registered Charity No. 1038333
A company limited by guarantee. Registered in England No. 2931892

Contents

Foreword   vii

Introduction   ix

Getting them on board

1	Writing job advertisements	3
2	Executive search	10
3	CVs	17
4	Selection interviews	24
5	Psychometric tests	32
6	Assessment centres	39
7	Using references	47
8	Induction programmes	55

Signing them up

9	Employment contracts	65
10	Fixed-term contracts	73
11	Annual hours contracts	80
12	Managing expatriates	88

Putting them on the payroll

13	Salary surveys	99
14	Job evaluation schemes	105
15	Salary structures	112
16	Rewarding performance	119

17 Flexible benefits   127
18 Childcare assistance   134
19 Company cars   141

Training them up
20 Identifying training needs   151
21 Management training providers   160
22 Training methods   168
23 Management games   175
24 Evaluating training   181
25 Preparation for retirement   188

Foreword

All too often the glut of information that seems to come at us from every direction in this digital age is accompanied by a famine of wisdom. The field of managing and developing people is no exception. A bewildering range of books, learned journals, professional magazines, specialist bulletins, training packages and now on-line information services competes for our attention. It has become difficult even for the conscientious student to keep up-to-date with the latest thinking, and well-nigh impossible for the busy manager.

With so many authors appearing as guides to people management, a new role has become necessary – someone to act as a guide to the guides. A person specification might read as follows: someone with wide practical experience of every aspect of managing people, in several sectors and at both operational and strategic levels. Someone with the intellectual curiosity to search out new ideas and the analytical skills to put them in context. Someone who is in touch with a wide variety of HR and other managers, and knows their current concerns. And, perhaps most important, someone who has a talent for expression and loves to write.

Alan Fowler fits this specification in every respect. His formal studies included the one-year personnel management course at the London School of Economics in the 1950s, and an Open University degree in Social Sciences in the 1970s. His professional career included spells with Clarks Shoes, the Nigerian Sugar Company, Costain Construction, the Greater London Council and then Hampshire County Council, where he headed a combined personnel and management services department for ten years. In 1987 he was made a Companion of the former Institute of Personnel Management (now the IPD), and also became a freelance consultant. He has since worked with many different private- and public-sector clients. He has written a dozen books, many for the IPD, regularly contributes to *People Management* and *Local Government Chronicle*, teaches a diploma course and, until very recently, has been active as an employers'-side member on industrial tribunals.

He had already been contributing to *Personnel Management* magazine for many years before his monthly 'How To' series began. It was quickly apparent he had found his forte as the guide to the guides. Reader research and informal feedback showed 'How To' to be one of the most popular features of the magazine, so it was natural it should become a regular item in *People Management* (successor to *Personnel Management*) from its launch in 1995. Yet the principles and techniques Fowler describes so lucidly are of deep relevance to many besides HR and development professionals. His articles have now been collected into these two volumes, updated wherever necessary, providing a rich seam of material to this wider readership.

Rob MacLachlan, Editor, *People Management*

Introduction

Effective management of people lies at the heart of all major corporate initiatives. It is easy for directors to issue edicts that their companies must become more customer-focused, more quality-conscious or genuinely open to talent from all backgrounds, any of which can indeed make the difference between success and failure in the marketplace. Yet exhortation is never enough. If I have learned one thing from my long experience as a practitioner and consultant, it is that these inspiring ideals become realities only when employers find ways to:

- create a supportive corporate climate
- recruit people who possess – or can rapidly acquire – appropriate competencies
- communicate the key messages, in concrete practical terms, to all employees
- build strong teams, set challenging objectives and constantly monitor progress against targets
- reward the right behaviour while discouraging – and, where necessary, disciplining – 'wrong-doing'
- provide focused and cost-effective training in the key skills

▓ cope constructively with conflict without demotivating staff.

Taken on its own, it might not seem to matter much if staff returning from sick leave are treated as malingerers, if a major health and safety initiative is misspelled, dog-eared and tacked up on an untidy notice-board, or if a company car scheme makes half the managers feel under-valued. Yet the cumulative impact of such policies (or lack of policy) will be an environment in which commitment and enthusiasm never flourish. Only people can add essential value to an organisation's inanimate resources of money, equipment, material and information. Effective employers realise this and so devote much of their time and energy to maximising this contribution. In the long term, even the tiniest details of a payment system or an appraisal scheme will make a real impact on how people behave. And that is why I firmly believe employers should always pursue best practice in people management, whether or not they use the services of a dedicated personnel department or expert.

Together with its companion volume, *Get More – and More Results – from Your People,* this book brings together 50 articles that I originally wrote for the IPD's fortnightly magazine *People Management* (or its predecessors *Personnel Management* and *PM Plus*). All have stood the test of time and remain highly relevant today, although they have been updated where necessary to take account of recent legal or other environmental changes. (Most sections also include useful addresses and/or details of books by the IPD or other publishers for readers who wish to pursue individual topics in greater depth.) Each formed part of a long-running and continuing series of 'how to' pieces designed to provide quick reference guides to good practice across the full range of people management techniques. I have been delighted by their popularity with both HR students and professionals, although the key messages are equally essential for line managers in smaller or devolved organisations who have day-to-day responsibility for many aspects of people management.

This volume provides important insights for anyone involved in recruitment, selection, training and reward. Getting the right people on board, providing them with a package of benefits that helps to motivate and retain them, and ensuring they are developed throughout their working lives – these represent at least half the spectrum of essential people management skills. They are not, of course, the whole story – hence the need for a companion volume. But any organisation that gets selection, benefits and training right will have gone a long way towards getting more – and more value – from its people.

Getting them on board

1   Writing job advertisements

The cost of advertising a vacancy, using display advertisements in the national media, can be £10,000 or more for a senior appointment, and getting value for money is then of obvious importance. But whatever the cost, even for low-price advertisements in the local press, the key issue is whether the advertisement produces applicants of adequate number and calibre. This is dependent primarily on the words used and how they are displayed – the copy and the design.

Many organisations consider this to be a task for advertising experts and therefore use the services of advertising agencies. The quality of advertisements produced by agencies is generally high, and their use is certainly to be commended. But personnel managers still need to be involved, particularly to ensure that agency-designed advertisements accurately reflect the nature and style of their organisations and give the necessary emphasis to the qualities being sought. Some personnel managers write detailed copy themselves and use agencies only for graphic design and to handle advertising administration. Much of the advertising in local media is also produced in-house.

The main points to consider in writing advertisements or vetting suggested designs and copy from an agency are:

- the general image
- what information to include
- what to emphasise.

The image

Two main factors influence the general image of an advertisement. The first is that it should project an accurate image of the organisation. A bright, breezy advertisement with pop art imagery that might suit an informal, opportunistic company would probably be inappropriate for a regulatory public body. Job advertisements form part of, and should be consistent with, an organisation's corporate image.

Secondly, there should be a match between the nature of the job and the way it is portrayed in the advertisement. A job involving creativity and imagination is not best publicised by an advertisement that lacks design impact and uses administrative jargon. Technical jargon has a legitimate use, but only when it is relevant to the job, accurate and up-to-date. Personnel managers may need to check the use of technical phraseology with their professional colleagues.

The information to include

Job advertisements need to include information on five topics:

- the organisation
- the job

- selection criteria
- salary and benefits
- how to apply.

How much needs to be said about the organisation depends on how well known it is to potential applicants. The company which is a brand leader in the specialist field in which it is advertising may not need to use expensive advertising space explaining its achievements: its name may suffice. But organisations that are seeking applicants from outside their own field or are less well known would do well to describe themselves. Nothing very elaborate is needed: one sentence can often encapsulate the key features. For example: 'XYZ is a fast-growing, six-year-old company with a turnover of £5 million, specialising in the design and manufacture of control instrumentation for the bio-chemical industry'.

The two main features of the job in which applicants are interested are, first, the nature of the work and, secondly, why it is being advertised (e.g. is it a new job?). If the job is a direct replacement for someone who has left, there is little point in emphasising this. However, many jobs are advertised for other reasons, which are worth stating because they form part of the potential attraction. Two examples are: ' We are expanding our after-sales service teams as part of a customer-care programme' and 'Recent restructuring has given more commercial responsibility to local managers'.

Of even more importance is a thumbnail description of what the job entails. Job titles alone rarely provide an adequate picture. Potential applicants want to know what they would actually do if they had the job, so generalised statements such as 'responsible for achieving production targets' are not satisfactory. Examples of more specific descriptions are: 'Leading a team of 12 engineers in the design of marine components and liaising with sales and production in determining specifications'; or 'Handling correspondence and appointments for three senior managers: supervising a pool of word-processor operators'.

The job's location is of critical importance. It may also be helpful to indicate if considerable travelling is involved; both points can be covered in a few words such as: 'Basingstoke-based, with frequent travel throughout southern counties'.

It is a disadvantage to receive dozens of applications which fail to meet the criteria that are to be used in selection. The advertisement should therefore be as specific as possible about any essential requirements, and indicate desirable – though not necessarily essential – factors. If this proves difficult, it is probably because inadequate attention has been given to the person specification.

A single sentence can set the selection parameters without being unduly restrictive; for example: 'You will be a graduate, preferably in a scientific or engineering discipline, with a record of achievement over at least three years of developing client contacts in the process or construction industries'.

Many advertisements specify qualities such as 'enthusiasm', or 'drive'. Together with the description of jobs as 'challenging', these words have become advertising clichés, and do little to inform or attract applicants.

Salary is a key element in attracting suitable applicants, and there are very few situations justifying vague phrases such as 'salary commensurate with the responsibilities of the post'. Potential applicants need at least a ballpark figure, though not necessarily the precise details. Public-sector advertisements are often unduly complex, eg 'Salary grade PO3, £20,995 to £23,089 (pay award pending)'. Two much simpler alternatives are: 'Salary c. £21-23K' or 'Salary up to c. 23K'. Full details of the pay range, entry points and pending increases can be given in a supplementary information pack.

A similar point applies to other benefits. Applicants are not necessarily impressed by a lengthy list including such minutiae as subsidised canteen, payment of professional fees or free car-parking. It all depends on the job. The canteen and car-parking might be very important to clerical jobs in a town centre, but irrelevant to a managerial post in which the three key points are salary, share options and car. Some reference to relocation payments may be useful, while training and career development opportunities can also be important. In general, though, it is the job, rather than the benefits (other than salary level), which attracts applicants.

There are three things applicants need to know about processing an application. The first is whether more information is available before a formal application has to be submitted. It is consequently helpful to state: 'To find out more, telephone John Smith on . . .' or 'Phone . . . for an information pack' – or some similar formula. Secondly, they need to know whether they need to submit a letter and/or CV or to complete an application form. It is extremely irritating for an applicant to prepare and send a CV, only to be sent an application form. If forms are to be used, the advertisement should state 'Telephone . . . for an application form'. Alternatively, it should say something like: 'Write enclosing full personal and career details.' Thirdly, applicants need to know whether there is a closing date – a common practice in the public sector, though used less often in the private sector.

What to emphasise

For most people, the four most important points that influence a decision to reply to job advertisement are the advertiser (is this an organisation in which I would like to work?); the job (is it interesting?); the location (is it somewhere I would like to live or which I can travel to daily?); and the salary level (does it pay enough?).

All these points can be emphasised in the headings, so that they catch the eye of the person scanning appointment pages. A typical example is:

IT SYSTEMS MANAGER
Birmingham: c. £35,000 + car

with a prominent company name and logo within the design. These headings can then be expanded in the text of the advertisement.

Slogans and illustrations can be used to highlight specific characteristics of the work. Award-winning advertisements for police, nurses and the armed forces have all portrayed difficult work situations under an attention-drawing headline – a recognition that an important attraction for good applicants is work that involves effort and initiative.

But as a general rule it is unwise to use slogans without expert advice from a good agency. For the in-house copywriter, the straightforward job/location/salary formula is a safer, well-proven option. The text of the advertisement should be clear, concise and follow a logical sequence. With space at a premium, the aim should be to make every word count. The two key qualities in copywriting are clarity and precision.

Further reading

Courtis J. *Recruitment Advertising*. London, Institute of Personnel and Development, 1994.

2   Executive search

The use of executive search consultants (popularly known as headhunters) has become a common form of recruitment – primarily for senior appointments – despite reservations being expressed at times about the ethics and costs of the search process. Proponents of executive search stress that, as with any form of consultancy, it is for the client to specify and monitor the standards of the service sought, while costs need be no higher than those of a widely advertised vacancy handled in-house.

The circumstances in which executive search is most useful include:

- when it is thought that potential candidates may exist who are interested in a change of job but are probably reluctant to respond formally to an open advertisement. Senior managers are often understandably wary of upsetting their relationships with their current employers and may not be wholly confident about the confidentiality of a formal application. They also need to know more about the vacancy before committing themselves to a possible job change. They are much more likely to respond to either a direct approach by a headhunter or to an advertisement placed by a headhunter which guarantees an informal, confidential discussion with the consultant before an application is formalised.

- when potential candidates are known to exist, but are probably not seeking a career move. Experience shows that some managers who will not respond to any form of advertising do become interested in a possible new job if approached personally by an executive search consultant.

- when it is necessary to recruit someone from a sector, or with a skill, in which the organisation has little experience. A headhunter with such experience and contacts may then be of great assistance in identifying and contacting possible candidates and advising on their suitability.

- when it is difficult for the organisation to handle the recruitment and selection process in-house. Typically, this occurs when a chief executive is being recruited and it is considered inappropriate for the personnel manager to be seen to play a major role in the selection of his or her future boss.

Selecting a headhunter

Having decided to use executive search, the first step is to select the consultant. The main formal sources of information about executive search consultants are the professional associations and the directory listed at the end of this chapter. Informally, recommendations from colleagues in other organisations are very helpful in choosing a shortlist of consultants.

The selection of a shortlist should be influenced by the level and nature of the post to be filled. Some headhunters deal only with very senior appointments in the £100,000 salary range and upwards. More will accept assignments for jobs in the £40,000-plus range, while small local consultancies may take on jobs down to about £25,000. There is then a choice between generalists or specialists, with some headhunters concentrating on particular functions, such as finance or purchasing, or operating mainly in one sector, such as the City.

Having identified four or five likely consultants, each should be contacted to see if they are interested in submitting a formal bid for the contract. At this stage the only information they will need is a brief outline of the job and its salary range. Those headhunters expressing an interest in the assignment should then be invited to attend for a detailed briefing. The information the client should provide and explain at this meeting includes a job description; a preliminary person specification; salary range and other major benefits; why the vacancy exits; general background about the organisation (its size, function, structure and culture); any organisations that are off-limits for the search (there may be companies from which it is considered inappropriate to draw candidates); any specific requirements (eg equal opportunity objectives); and the desired timescale.

Each consultant should provide information about their own organisation (size, history, achievements); their methods of working (eg the extent to which they would use a candidate databank and/or advertising to supplement the search); their normal fee and expense system; and any organisations that are off-limits for search (reputable headhunters will not contact staff of their other clients). They should also outline the likely timescales and name the consultant who will be conducting the search. To ensure compatibility, the client should insist on meeting the person who will actually handle the assignment. Each headhunter should then be asked to submit a proposal in writing, setting out their understanding of the assignment, how they propose to conduct it, their suggested timescale, fees and expenses, and any guarantees. A final choice of consultant can then be made, partly on the basis of the written proposals, partly on the impression gained through the briefing.

There are five important points to consider. The first is the person specification. Each consultant should submit their ideas for the person specification, drawn up in the light of all the information they have been given. This is a good test of how well each has understood the client's requirements and style.

Secondly, there are timescales: these should indicate how long it will take them to produce a list of suitable candidates. Somewhere between four and 10 weeks would be normal.

The third point is advertising. It may be suggested that advertising is used to supplement search, and in parts of the public sector, advertising is a statutory requirement. It should be clear from the outset whether the consultant or the client is to handle this advertising, whether it will identify the client, and whether the costs are to be included in the consultant's quoted fees, or treated as an expense item.

Fourthly, there is the question of fees and expenses. Assignments are rarely awarded solely on the basis of fees, as there is generally little difference between head-hunters on this score. The most common level of fees is one-third of the appointee's initial annual salary – although it is important to specify whether this is base salary, or salary plus allowances or bonuses. Some consultants quote a fixed fee based on their assessment of the work involved, but this is often very close to one-third of annual salary. Expenses can add considerably to the total cost, and some consultants will guarantee a top limit of, say, 15 per cent of the fee. Provision should be made for the client to approve any major items in advance.

The final point is guarantees. Headhunters offer a variety of these. Some will undertake to continue a search until a suitable candidate is appointed, regardless of how long this may take. Many will resume a search without further fees if the initial appointee proves unsatisfactory or leaves within six months. The small print on these guarantees needs to be studied with care.

Working with a headhunter

Once a headhunter has been selected, it is essential that a close working partnership is established. Unless there are very pressing reasons to prevent it, the consultant should meet the prospective appointee's future colleagues, perhaps attend a management meeting, and tour the organisation to pick up its values and culture. It will also be necessary to agree a number of issues:

- the final person specification, which is the key to a successful assignment. This needs very intensive discussion, particularly with the manager to whom the appointee will report, and must cover not only the know-how and experience that is being sought but also the desirable personality characteristics. An effective headhunter may be able to suggest constructive amendments to the client's initial specification, while the client must also be very specific about any key requirements.

- the range of target organisations and contacts the headhunter will pursue. The client should be assured of the thoroughness of the search.

- the selection methods the headhunter will use. The client should know of, and approve, the use of psychometric tests or other selection techniques – potential candidates will be influenced in their view of the post and the client organisation by the way the headhunter operates.

- the information the headhunter will give prospective candidates about the client organisation. In a sense, the consultant will be acting as a representative of the client, and it is essential that accurate information is given to prospective candidates about the organisation they may eventually work for.

- the number of candidates the client wishes ideally to be submitted for final selection. To be given too many – say, over six – will indicate that the consultant is not being sufficiently thorough: to be told there are only two may be thought to offer inadequate choice.

- how references are to be obtained. The headhunter should be expected to make all necessary checks on the shortlisted candidates, but the client may wish to pursue further inquiries.

Once the assignment starts, the headhunter should keep in contact with the client, report general progress and check on any points arising from preliminary contacts with potential candidates. Although confidentiality of candidates' identity may need to be maintained at this stage, it is important that the client should be asked whether the consultant should proceed with a candidate who does not wholly meet the agreed specification but whom the headhunter considers potentially suitable.

Finally, arrangements need to be agreed about processing the names on the headhunter's shortlist. Are these to be submitted as and when they are identified or (as is more usual) put forward as a group at the end of the search? What form of report on these candidates does the client require? Is the client or the headhunter to make the final interview arrangements? Will the headhunter attend and advise the client at these interviews? A working partnership between client and consultant throughout the assignment is the key to the effective use of executive search.

Further information

1 *Executive Grapevine* (directory of executive search consultants).

2 Association of Search and Selection Consultants: 36–38 Mortimer Street, London, W1N 7RB (0171 323 4300).

3 JONES S. *The Headhunting Business*. London, Macmillan, 1989.

3   CVs

Personnel managers have several interests in CVs. They are often the first source of information about job applicants; advice on writing them may be given to employees as part of redundancy counselling; and personnel managers need to produce their own CVs when job-hunting. A guide to the best use of CVs in recruitment is also a useful aid in writing your own.

When drafting job advertisements it is important to state whether CVs are required or whether applicants should write or telephone for application forms. Such forms ensure that all the relevant information is supplied in a standard format, which eases the task of making an initial assessment of a large number of applications. The main advantage of CVs over application forms is that they demonstrate an applicant's ability to present information clearly and to project personal qualities.

Career counsellors often advise redundant staff to provide only a job-specific résumé of favourable career information. Most outplacement advice emphasises that CVs are marketing documents, not comprehensive factual inventories. This is fine for the speculative application, but not in reply to a job advertisement where the employer requires a full personal and job history. If comprehensive details are needed, but application forms are not to be used, it is a good idea to say so in the job advertisement.

There are other procedures. Applicants may be asked simply to supply a CV of unspecified type in the first instance. From these CVs, many of which are likely to be résumés, the most interesting applicants are selected for more detailed consideration and are sent application forms before an interviewing shortlist is compiled. Alternatively, CVs may be used for shortlisting, with application forms issued only to candidates invited to interview. If CVs are relied on for the whole selection process, it may still be necessary for the successful candidate to complete some form of questionnaire to provide the full details needed for the personnel records system.

When advising redundant employees about job applications, it helps to distinguish between the résumé and the comprehensive CV. Both need to be clearly laid out and to be as concise as possible, but the former can be much more selective than the latter, highlighting relevant personal and career achievements. Employees should be advised that, as a rough guide, the résumé is best kept to one page, the full CV to two. Busy personnel managers know only too well the time problem of assessing a large number of responses to a job advertisement, while the speculative application needs to catch the attention as soon as it is scanned.

The comprehensive CV, when this type of document is requested in job advertisements, should be modelled to some extent on best practice in application form design. The information is best set out in clearly labelled sections, generally in this order:

- personal details: full name, address, telephone numbers (daytime and evening), age and date of birth. It may be argued that age is irrelevant, but unless and until age discrimination is made unlawful it remains, unfortunately, a factor most employers want to know about. To omit it may simply draw attention to its omission. Giving details of marital status is a different matter. Although many application forms still ask for these details, discrimination on such grounds is unlawful. In CVs, these details can safely be omitted.
- education. Some discretion can be exercised as to how much detail to supply. Except at graduate-entry level, it is normally sufficient to give only very brief details of education from age 16 to 18, with more details of higher education and particularly of diplomas, certificates and degrees, including the university attended and the class of degree. Lists of GCSE O-levels should be avoided and A-level details included only if they really add useful information.
- professional qualifications. It may be worthwhile specifying not only the qualification (with the NVQ level if appropriate) and the awarding institution, but also how it was obtained – eg by part-time or full-time study.
- current or last employment. It is the most recent job history which is normally of primary interest to a prospective employer. It may therefore be helpful to

highlight this in a section of its own and to give more details than for earlier jobs. If the job advertisement asks for salary information, give the current or final salary but also the job's salary range if this shows a higher grade maximum. Do not inflate salary details, though average bonuses or performance payments can be given. Remember that if the employer seeks references, the salary data may be checked.

- previous employment history. Jobs should be listed with dates (any gap in chronology is likely to be questioned) but with a diminishing amount of information for the earlier job history. Do not waste space by detailing early and irrelevant jobs.

- training and development. It is not advisable to give a long list of all the training courses and seminars that have been attended, but some training and development information may be helpful. Management training courses of a week or more should normally be listed, together with any training in relevant specialist skills.

- personal interests/activities. It is not essential to include this section, particularly if all that can be said is something like 'normal family activities and gardening'. However, if there are aspects that provide evidence of relevant knowledge, skills or personality, these are worth listing. Examples might include being a school governor, running a computer club, or various forms of voluntary work, which demonstrate organisational and management skills. An unusual hobby such as skydiving or genealogical research can be worth mentioning, even though it has no obvious relevance to the job, as it may help to give the CV an interesting feature which the reader remembers.

Application forms often ask for a statement about the reasons for an interest in the job, and include a blank section for any other comments. When CVs are used, comments of this kind are best made in a covering letter, rather than in the CV itself. This letter can also highlight those elements of job experience that are particularly relevant. All these comments need to be succinct and factual. It does no good to make generalised claims such as 'I am confident I have all the qualities needed to be successful in this appointment.' The covering letter should concentrate on whatever factor will distinguish the application from others. In marketing terms, what is the unique selling point?

The comprehensive CV may be appropriate for applications for almost any job. Résumé-type CVs, on the other hand, are often most effective when they are tailored to match the characteristics and probable interests of each targeted organisation. For example, if an approach is being made to a retail company but only one of three past jobs has been in that sector, that is the job to describe in the most detail. The general style of the CV may also be influenced by the sector of the organisation to which it is addressed. Applications to marketing organisations or to parts of the publishing industry may make an effective impact if the style and layout indicates a flair for lively prose or an interest in graphic design. To use the same approach for, say, a financial institution or a local authority might have an adverse effect.

Many outplacement consultants suggest placing a short personal profile at the head of this type of CV; for example: 'A personnel generalist, 30, professionally qualified, with eight years varied experience in two major manufacturing companies. A record of achievement, particularly in the implementation of employee communications and performance-management systems. Now ready for a strategic HR role.' This type of profile needs to be used with considerable caution. It has become somewhat of a CV cliché, and some employers now assume that if this style is adopted, its drafting has probably been aided by a careers counsellor and is not the sole effort of the applicant. Some personnel managers even claim they can identify which particular outplacement consultancy has been involved.

Unless a profile can be written in a more lively or personalised style than this example, it may be better to use a condensed and more selective version of the detailed CV. This would omit some of the less important details, while emphasising the most important or favourable career elements, using short, bullet-pointed phrases rather than narrative. It can be more radical than the detailed CV in grouping early or less relevant jobs together with very little detail, and need only describe the most noteworthy qualifications. If this type of CV interests readers but leaves them wanting to know more, that could be an advantage. It may result in a telephone call or an invitation to come in for an informal discussion. The CV's objective is not, by itself, to obtain an offer of employment; it is to open the door to personal contact with a prospective employer.

CVs of both types must be in typescript or print, not

hand-written. The clearest possible typeface should be used – laser or bubble-jet printing is preferable to dot matrix if it is word-processed. It is advisable to use the same typeface for the CV and the covering letter. A CV in a different typeface may give the impression it has been produced by a commercial CV-writing service. A common fault with word processing is to use too many different typefaces and sizes, resulting in a fussy overall appearance. A single typeface with a maximum of two different forms of heading or emphasis is all that is needed. Similar restraint is advisable if a colour printer is used, when just one other colour than black, used solely for the main section headings, is probably best.

Further information

COURTIS J. *Getting a Better Job.* London, Institute of Personnel and Development, 1993.

4 Selection interviews

Despite a growing range of techniques such as psychometric testing and bio-analysis, interviews continue to hold their own as the standard method of selection. This is despite research evidence which casts significant doubts on their predictive validity. The British Psychological Society quotes predictive validity coefficients (see p35) of 0.25 for structured interviews and zero for unplanned interviews using the normal statistical scale of 0 (no relationship between interview predictions and reality) to 1.0 (100 per cent accuracy). On these figures, even well-conducted interviews are only 25 per cent better than sticking a pin in a list of candidates.

Yet most managers, whether or not they are experienced interviewers, feel instinctively that the judgements they make when interviewing are more reliable than this. Or to put it another way, few managers would feel confident about appointing a candidate without an interview, even with extensive positive indications from techniques such as job simulations, which the BPS claims achieve far higher validity scores. There is something about the face-to-face interaction of an interview which meets a very powerful psychological need to see and hear a candidate before entering into an employment commitment. What is clear from research, regardless of precise validity ratings, is that well-planned and well-conducted interviews produce very much better results than unstructured questioning.

There are four main elements or stages of the good interview:

- preparation
- sequence and timing
- questioning techniques
- analysing the result.

Preparation

Interview training sometimes concentrates wholly on the techniques of questioning and listening, but unless the interview has been prepared, follows the most effective sequence, and its results are considered systematically, some of the benefits of a sound technique will be lost. Two documents are essential when preparing for an interview – the person specification and the application form or CV. The fact that a candidate has been selected for interview implies that on the documentary evidence there is a reasonable match between the application data and the person specification, but it is rare for this match to be perfect.

One element of preparation is therefore to note those features of the application which seem weakest against the specification, so these can be probed more deeply. The application data should also be studied for any missing items, or for entries that require more explanation than the candidate has provided in writing. These may include time periods not covered by the employment, reasons for changing jobs (the brief reasons given on an application form rarely tell the whole story) and descriptions of previous experience which seem potentially of considerable interest (for or against selection) but which are too abbreviated.

There are also aspects to explore at interview – such as personality and attitude – which cannot be deduced satisfactorily from a CV, though some hints may be given by the style of covering letters or sections in the application form in which candidates are invited to comment on their interest in the job.

There are two key questions to answer in matching the application documents against the specification:

- What more do I need to find out or check at the interview to be sure the candidate meets the essential selection criteria, or does not fail because of a disqualifying factor?
- What further information should be obtained at the interview to ensure I have an accurate picture of how well the candidate meets the desirable and useful, though not wholly essential, criteria?

If other selection techniques, such as psychometric tests, are being used, and these have been administered before the interview, they may have produced pointers to matters worth investigating more thoroughly during the interview. For example, is the candidate really as independently minded or as sociable as the personality test may have suggested? The effective interviewer will make a note of all these points, probably in the form of questions to be asked, before going on to consider the best sequence for the interview.

Sequence and timing

Apart from the nature of the beginning and the end of an interview, there is no single best sequence to follow. Some interviewers prefer to go through the candidate's history chronologically, some work backwards from the current job, others may choose to examine various aspects in turn, but not necessarily in date order – work, education, outside interests, personal circumstances and so on. What is important is to decide in advance what sequence to follow, and which elements within the sequence are of most importance.

A very common failing is to spend too long in the earlier stages of the interview on matters which are not of central importance and then run out of time to probe as thoroughly as is needed into really key issues. So part of the process of deciding the sequence is to allocate at least a rough time span for each section.

All interviews should have a satisfactory start and finish. At the beginning, the candidate should be invited into the room and shown where to sit. The interviewer should welcome the candidate by name and make a self-introduction. Two or three minutes of ice-breaking small talk is advisable before launching into the serious interview ('Did you have a good journey?', 'Have you been to this town before?'). The aim is quickly to put the candidate (and the interviewer) as much at ease as is possible in what is potentially a stressful situation.

There are three elements to the closing stage: first, find

out whether the interviewee has anything they would like to say about themselves which did not come out in the rest of the interview; secondly, ask them if they have any questions; and thirdly, thank them for coming, tell them that you have enjoyed the discussion and say you will be contacting them to tell them the outcome in a certain number of days.

Questioning techniques

All interview training stresses the importance of using open-ended questions – those which cannot be answered yes or no. While this is undoubtedly excellent advice, it is by no means the whole story: effective interviewing requires the use of several other types of questions, including the closed question, and the open question sometimes has limitations. For example, the question: 'What has been the main feature of your work in recent months?' (an open question) may result in either a one-word reply ('Marketing'), or an overlong explanation describing a complex project in inordinate detail. Either way, some other form of questioning would be necessary to make effective progress.

So in addition to open-ended questioning, the following types of questions need to be used:

▪ probing questions – to provide a clearer focus to too short or too generalised answers. If the answer to: 'What has been your most important achievement in your current job?' is: 'Starting a technical information service', a first probing question might be: 'Tell us what work this involved.' Poor interviewers too often let a candidate's general and uninformative answer pass without a probe, simply because they are working through a list of prepared open questions.

- closed questions – to clarify a point of fact. The answers to questions about the technical information service may omit one key point, which a simple closed question will elucidate: 'Were you the project leader?'

- play-back questions – testing the interviewer's understanding of what has been said (and the clarity of the candidate's answers) by playing back to the candidate what he or she appears to have told you. For example: 'Are you saying that you found this project extremely difficult to handle because of its technical content?' If the candidate says something like 'Well, not exactly', this needs to be followed by a probe – 'Tell me what the real difficulty was.'

- hypothetical questions – putting a situation to the candidate and asking how he or she would respond. This type of question needs to be considered with care: it is unfair to expect a candidate to give a detailed answer to a problem which requires a greater knowledge of the context than the candidate can be expected to have. But some such questions, lying well within the candidate's experience or expertise, can be illuminating.

There are two forms of questioning to avoid:

- multiple questions, such as: 'What difficulties did you have with this project and were they technical or did you run into time problems?' The likelihood is the candidate will answer only one item, or will become confused about the real point of the question.

■ leading questions, which appear to be looking for one particular answer: 'Don't you think you would have found less difficulty if you had involved a technician in the project?' Questions should never give any hint of the type of response the interviewer may consider good or bad.

For this reason, too, interviewers should avoid commenting on candidates' answers, unless this is being done intentionally to stimulate further discussion. If you strongly disagree with something the candidate has said, stay mum unless the answer needs to be probed.

Analysing the result

However good the interview has been, its value will be diminished if the results are not analysed systematically. Too often interviewers jump to a general conclusion based on their immediate and subjective feeling about how the interview has gone.

For most jobs, the important point is not whether the candidate has been a pleasant and articulate interviewee, but how well the information that has been obtained (objective and qualitative) matches the specification. Some interviewers use the well-known seven- or five-point plans for this purpose, and allot marks out of ten for each element (attainments, disposition, circumstances, etc.) This is a questionable practice. The best use of these standard interview plans is as a checklist in producing the specification and in interview preparation. In the final stage, what is important is not a mechanistic total score against a set number of very general factors, but how well the candidate matched the very specific requirements of the particular job. A better plan, therefore, is to list the essential, desirable and useful criteria in the specification and mark each candidate against these.

Different criteria (apart from those that are genuinely essential) will probably need to be given different weightings, and shrewd judgement may be needed in choosing between two or more generally suitable candidates. To what extent, for example, might technical know-how beyond the essential be considered more valuable than a particular personality characteristic? Making such judgements after the interview is as important as the conduct of the interview itself, and the important point is that such judgements should be rational, explicable and uninfluenced by irrelevancies or prejudice.

Further reading

1 HACKETT P. *The Selection Interview.* London, Institute of Personnel and Development, 1995.
2 MacKay I. *Asking Questions.* London, Institute of Personnel and Development, 1995.

5   Psychometric tests

There has been a steady growth in recent years in the use of psychometric tests, primarily to assist selection and assessment. There has also been a proliferation of the types and numbers of tests being marketed – not all of which justify the claims of their producers. To select and use tests effectively, it is necessary to establish the qualities or characteristics to be assessed, and to check the validity of tests that claim to produce such data. Once the right test is found, it must be administered with skill and the results married with other relevant information before firm conclusions are made.

It may seem obvious to suggest that before any test is used a decision is needed about the information it is required to produce and how this relates to selection or assessment decisions. When tests are used to identify specific aptitudes, this is rarely a problem. If a job requires a high level of numeracy, a test can establish this. Unfortunately, personality questionnaires are often used without hard evidence of the links between specific personality characteristics and performance standards in particular kinds of work. A test may indicate that a candidate is introverted, has creative ability, thinks analytically and tends more to pragmatism than idealism. This may be interesting, but what evidence is there to link this combination of characteristics to success or failure in the type of work for which the candidate is being considered? Reliance on norm tables (average scores for people in particular occupations) may result in selection decisions that screen out unconventional high-flyers and reinforce mediocrity.

Consequently, test selection should start by addressing the following questions:

- What qualities or characteristics have been shown to correlate with high or low performance standards in the relevant job?
- Are there any valid tests that will help to identify and assess these qualities?

Test types

Psychometric tests are often categorised as assessing either ability (cognitive tests) or personality. This may be expanded into three main types:

- tests of specific ability, for example numeracy, verbal and spatial perception
- tests of general mental ability (sometimes described as tests of general intelligence): for example, analytical reasoning, critical thinking ability
- psychometric questionnaires, for example general personality tests; tests for specific personality traits such as values, interest preferences, learning styles and team types.

Another form of categorisation distinguishes between normative tests (those for which an individual's results can be compared with the average score for a population), and ipsative tests (broadly, when the results are descriptive rather than scored).

Test validity

Decisions about the specific characteristics for which tests are to be used will narrow the choice to one or other of these broad categories. The search can then begin for the most appropriate test or tests. This task is not eased by the proliferation of tests on the market, particularly those that claim to identify specific characteristics such as leadership, honesty, negotiating ability or commercial aptitude. The main issue is a test's validity, although this has several dimensions.

Face validity is concerned with how relevant the test appears to be for the particular job or type of work. Will it be acceptable to candidates who may lack confidence in, or resent, a test that seems to ask irrelevant or intrusive questions? Some of the personality questionnaires originally designed for use in clinical psychiatry may lack face validity. *Content validity* is concerned with the extent to which the assessed factors are relevant to the work. Job content needs to be analysed and matched against test content to ensure that the test results will indicate the candidate's job suitability.

There are then two types of empirical validity – the ways in which the test has been shown in practice to predict job suitability or performance standards. *Concurrent validity* is determined by the test results of current job-holders and assesses the correlation between their test scores and levels of performance. If large numbers of sub-jects have been tested and certain correlations are strong, the results are usually a reliable basis for performance predictions. There is a risk, however, particularly with small numbers, that some positive correlations may be merely coincidental and that some patterns of scoring not represented in the sample may be better indications of success than those in the sample.

Predictive validity is the most important indicator. It requires a study of the performance of employees some time after they have been tested, and is concerned with the extent to which predictions of their performance made on the basis of test results have been confirmed in practice. Predictive validity is defined statistically by a coefficient that ranges between zero (correlation between test results and performance is no better than chance) and 1.0 (complete correlation). Of course, no test – or any other selection technique – ever achieves 1.0 and The British Psychological Society quotes typical values of 0.35 for cognitive tests and 0.15 for personality question-naires. These figures compare with 0.45 (the highest) for job-simulation exercises and 0.25 for structured inter-views. The low figure for personality tests has been challenged by some reputable test producers whose published data for their own tests give figures of between 0.2 and 0.5. But these higher figures need to be treated with caution where the number of subjects was small and the assessment of performance largely subjective.

Test producers should always be asked how and by whom their tests have been designed and the extent to which they have been tested. They should provide norm data if appropriate, and the validity coefficient of at least some actual test usages. They should be willing to say which organisations are using their tests and it is then helpful to contact these organisations about their experience of the tests. Producers unable or unwilling to provide such data should generally be avoided unless they are open about the untried nature of their tests and you are willing to use the tests experimentally.

There are two other factors to be considered when selecting a test. The first is the test's freedom from direct or indirect discriminatory bias. A number of tests designed many years ago have a marked gender bias, while tests of specific abilities may unwittingly discriminate against some ethnic minorities. Expert advice may be needed to identify such faults.

The other factor is practical one – the test's utility or cost-effectiveness. Some tests can be expensive and time-consuming to obtain, administer and interpret; others may be marketed as cheap and easy to run. For the busy personnel manager with a limited budget, there is an obvious attraction in quick, low-cost tests that require little training to administer and produce instant computerised assessments. There is no inverse correlation between cost and validity, but cheap computerised tests certainly need to be scrutinised before allowing their advantages to outweigh concerns about their validity. Equally, there is no point in committing time and money to tests, however eminent their general reputation, if they are irrelevant.

Test administration and use

Tests will not produce consistent or reliable results unless they are properly administered. Even apparently minor differences in the explanation and instructions given to test subjects, or the circumstances in which tests are taken, may affect results. Reputable test producers always provide detailed instructions, and these should be followed to the letter.

It is essential to check that candidates understand the procedure involved, particularly for computerised self-reporting tests. Most tests open with one or two unscored questions to ensure that candidates understand what they have to do and to get them over initial nervousness. Only persons trained and qualified to an appropriate standard should also undertake test interpretation. Reputable test producers are always specific about such qualifications and try to restrict the sale of their tests to properly trained users.

Because no test reaches 100 per cent validity (ie, a coefficient of 1.0), they should rarely be the sole basis of an appointment. The exception may be where meeting a measurable standard in one specific ability (perhaps numeracy) is the single crucial selection criterion and a test has proven reliable. Normally, test results need to be considered alongside an interview, previous employment history, references and, if possible, performance in job-simulation exercises. Test results that conflict with these other sources may indicate the need for further analysis or deeper probing at interview. Results that support other indications may resolve doubts or help to confirm favourable impressions. Because no single method can be wholly reliable, the extent to which different methods point in the same direction is a valuable aid to making reliable predictions.

Further Information

1 TOPLIS J., DULEWICZ V. *and* FLETCHER C. *Psychological Testing: A manager's guide.* 3rd edn. London, Institute of Personnel and Development, 1997.

2 THE BRITISH PSYCHOLOGICAL SOCIETY: St. Andrews House, 48 Princess Road East, Leicester, LE17 DR7.

6 Assessment centres

There have been many studies of selection techniques which show that no single method of assessment can achieve a high validity rating. However, the same studies indicate that job simulation exercises achieve a much higher validity rating than any other technique, and a combination of different techniques produces the best results of all. These findings largely explain the growth in the use of assessment centres over the past decade, and the nature of the assessment centre process itself.

In essence, an assessment centre consists of a small group of participants who undertake a series of tests and exercises under observation, with a view to the assessment of their skills or competencies, their suitability for particular roles, and their potential for development. Although the assessment methods often include standard techniques such as psychometric tests, the core of an assessment centre consists of a set of job simulation exercises. An assessment centre is not a place, but a process.

The purpose

There are three principal uses for an assessment centre, each requiring its own particular design elements. They are: graduate selection; selection for specific (normally managerial) appointments; and to aid internal promotion and development.

The main difference between graduate selection and selection for a specific vacancy is that the assessment exercises for the latter can be focused on the competencies required for that job, whereas for graduates a broader range of assessment is generally needed. In designing exercises for graduates, it also needs to be kept in mind that few will have had significant work experience, nor can a knowledge of management principles and practices be assumed.

When assessment centres are used for internal purposes, there is a much greater commonality of knowledge and attitude than with external candidates. Care needs to be taken, however, to avoid the results of a job simulation exercise being biased by any one participant having specialist experience in the type of work being simulated. Some participants may also attempt to predict and display the characteristics they expect the in-house assessors (whom they may know well) will be looking for.

Skills and competencies

No assessment centre can be successful unless a correct analysis has first been made of the particular skills and competencies which it is designed to identify. An otherwise highly professional centre will fail if it is effective in highlighting certain competencies but which are not of central relevance to job performance.

For example, in one centre to select sales executives it was assumed that a key quality was sociability, and exercises were designed to test for this. Later research showed this factor was irrelevant to sales success and that what should have been tested were qualities of independence and persistence. Developments in the identification of competencies (eg within the Management Charter Initiative) should help to ensure that the skills and aptitudes an assessment centre is designed to reveal are those that are central to high job performance in the particular kind of work participants are being assessed for.

Tests and techniques

An essential feature of an assessment centre is the use of a range of assessment methods rather then reliance on any one technique. It is therefore necessary to decide what to include in this assessment battery, and this largely determines the centre's duration.

A typical centre will occupy at least two days, as it is difficult to include a sufficient range of exercises in less time. These activities may include:

- structured interviews
- a self-assessment questionnaire
- psychometric tests
- in-tray exercises
- group discussions
- group problem-solving job simulations
- individual job-simulated tasks
- job-related role-play.

The balance between group and individual activities should be influenced by the nature of the jobs with which the assessments are concerned. If the organisation is one in which team working is dominant, the observation of participants will concentrate on performance in a group context. A different emphasis will be needed if the centre is to identify likely candidates for jobs of a more individual or isolated nature.

A decision is also needed about the amount of written exercises and individual oral presentations. Again, this must be determined by the competencies needed in the jobs for which the centre is designed. If skilful drafting under pressure is important in the work, this type of exercise should be included in the assessment centre – eg writing a press release on an emergency topic against a very tight deadline. Similarly, if the organisation makes frequent use of formal oral presentations within its decision-making processes, or the work involves making this kind of presentation to clients, exercises of this nature should be included in the assessment programme.

Job simulation exercises

Designing a job simulation exercise is not simple. Consider, for example, an in-tray exercise in which each participant is given a set of papers (typical letters, messages, memos) and asked to indicate how each item will be dealt with and in what order of priority.

In designing this exercise (as with all job simulations), the following criteria need to be met:

- It is a realistic test of relevant skills.
- The material can be understood by all the participants.
- The exercise can be completed in the time allocated.
- It can be systematically and consistently assessed.

It may be unwise to attempt to design job simulations without involving other managers. A better practice is to form a working group of several managers to produce ideas and raw material for these exercises; for the personnel or training manager to write the exercise and then refer it back to be vetted by the managers' group. The final version should then be test-run to ensure it meets the timing and other criteria.

The assessment process

In planning the assessment process, the three main factors to consider are:

- the list of competencies or other qualities to be assessed and how these are to be scored or rated
- the weighting to be given to each element and exercise. It might be decided, for example, that the result of a group problem-solving exercise should carry twice as much weight as the scores for a psychometric test.
- the form that the various assessments will take in order to ensure consistency of judgement and the prevention of bias or stereotyping.

The assessment decisions can be summarised on a rating grid (see table, below).

	Exercises and points scored					
Competence	Interview	In-tray exercise	Group problem	Group discussion	Psycho-metrics	Total score
	max:10	*max:10*	*max:30*	*max:15*	*max:15*	*max:80*
Organising						
Teamwork						
Leadership						
Analytical etc						

The assessors

While some of the assessments, such as psychometric test results, can be scored by standard methods, the core of the assessment centre is the observation of participants' performance on the various job simulations by a team of assessors.

It is normal for the panel of assessors to consist of line managers together with a personnel specialist who keeps overall control of proceedings. Some organisations find it helpful to include an external assessor – perhaps an occupational psychologist or training consultant. Most assessors need training in the assessment methodology. For each observed exercise there should be a schedule of the characteristics of behaviour and performance to be looked for, with guidance about how to record and rate them.

For example, in the observation of a group discussion, participants might be scored for factors such as:

- relevance of contributions
- degree of involvement
- originality of ideas
- influence on other group members.

The scores for these factors would be built up from entries recorded on an observation sheet while the group discussion proceeded. From these detailed scores, a broader rating can then be made for the key competencies listed on the overall rating grid.

Feedback

A decision must be made about the extent to which information about the assessments is relayed to and discussed with the participants. In a recruitment context this will probably be very limited, though it is much appreciated by candidates if the organisation can find the time at least to indicate the main assessment conclusions.

Where assessment centres are being used in a management development programme, feedback should be a major feature. Detailed advice can be given to each participant about their strong and weak points and about the action that might be taken by the individual and the organisation to build on strengths and correct weaknesses. Participants have an intense and understandable interest in how they have performed in the various exercises, and morale and confidence in the process will be damaged if there is any indication that it results in the production of secret reports.

Validation

Assessment centres are expensive, and may be counterproductive if the wrong competencies are assessed or if there are flaws in the assessment process. Very thorough analysis is essential, both of the process itself and of its outcomes, before a commitment is made to an ongoing programme of centres.

The factors to examine in validating a centre include:

- the assessors' and participants' immediate views
- whether the assessments make sense to the participants' managers and are confirmed by other evidence such as appraisal records
- in the longer term, the accuracy of assessment predictions
- whether the ratings display any significant

inconsistencies or bias. This may require statistical analysis of scores, particularly to examine variations in marking standards

■ whether any test or exercise was hard to administer or rate, or failed to differentiate between participants.

Further information

1 WOODRUFFE C. *Assessment Centres.* 2nd edn. London, Institute of Personnel and Development, 1994.

2 MUMFORD M. *Management Development.* 3rd edn. London, Institute of Personnel and Development, 1997.

3 PEARN KANDOLA. *Tools for Assessment and Development Centres.* London, Institute of Personnel and Development, 1996.

7 Using references

There are opposing views about the value of references. Some personnel managers argue that candidates nominate only referees they know will be supportive, so the resultant references are too bland and omit any adverse information. Those holding this view prefer to rely wholly on interviews and other selection techniques which, they feel, give more reliable insights into the strengths and weaknesses of candidates. Against this, many executive search consultants consider the thorough vetting of candidates' job records by reference to previous employers to be the single most important element in selection.

Critics of references usually base their view on the practice of requiring candidates to provide the names of two or three referees, who are then asked merely for a general reference, with no inquiries directed towards specific abilities. Some personnel managers criticise, on ethical grounds, the extensive vetting carried out by head-hunters, because it is conducted mainly by telephone (with no written proof of who said what) and occurs without the knowledge of candidates.

A more balanced approach avoids the extremes of the self-selected and generalised written reference, and of covert telephone vetting. Reference inquiries that are conducted with care and focused on key issues and fact-checking can play a useful part within a broad-based selection process. There are several issues to consider.

The legal position

Reference providers and users may be under the misapprehension that a reference labelled 'Strictly confidential' can, in all circumstances, be kept from the sight of its subject. In fact, if the reference becomes an issue in any legal action (eg for defamation or discrimination), a court or employment tribunal can order its disclosure. References may also become subject to disclosure under the 1998 Data Protection Act, whether stored in a manual or computerised form.

An occasional problem for the reference user is the excellent reference provided by a candidate's current employer, when in reality that employer is eager to lose the services of the employee. If such a candidate is appointed on the strength of a false reference of this kind and then proves unsatisfactory it is possible – at least in principle – to bring an action against the referee for the costs incurred as a result of the intentional deceit. In practice, the aim should be to avoid being misled by a reference of this kind, rather than incur the difficulties of an inappropriate appointment and the costs of unpredictable legal action. It should also be noted that if references are headed 'Without legal responsibility' or 'Without prejudice', the writers are saying, in effect, that they disclaim responsibility for any decisions the recipient may make as a result of the information they have given.

Contractual difficulties can arise if unsatisfactory references are received after offers of employment have been made and accepted. If a good reference from the current employer is considered essential but is deferred at the candidate's request until an offer can be made, the safest procedure is to make a provisional offer 'subject to satisfactory references'. If a bad reference is then given, the offer is not confirmed and no contractual liability arises.

If this provisional procedure is not followed and a firm offer has been accepted, its withdrawal on later receipt of a bad reference may result in the candidate becoming contractually entitled to payment in lieu of notice. However, if this withdrawal occurs because the reference reveals that the candidate has given false information, no claim for compensation is likely to be sustainable, as the candidate would have induced the offer through false pretences.

The only statutory limitation on references is the bar on the disclosure of spent convictions under the 1974 Rehabilitation of Offenders Act, and reference users must avoid seeking such information. There are exceptions to this legislation for some occupations (eg childcare work), but in these cases there are special procedures for checking criminal records which are critically important for this type of work but are outside the scope of this chapter.

Choosing the referees

The traditional method of referencing has been to require candidates to give the names of two or three persons from whom inquiries can be made. This is not an ideal approach if it constitutes the whole of the referencing procedure. Candidates will obviously select people who are likely to give them a favourable reference and omit those who may have more critical views. This is not to suggest abandoning the self-nomination of referees by candidates, as someone may be named who throws interesting light on aspects of the candidate's experience which are not apparent from the employment record. However, prospective employers need to consider whether the people nominated as referees by the candidate are capable of providing an adequate range of information. If not, they should add to the list.

In particular, a reference check is desirable from each of the candidate's previous employers, and the most useful information is likely to come from the candidate's immediate line managers, not necessarily from personnel managers. At interview, candidates can be asked the names of their previous managers and their agreement sought to references being obtained from these sources. Application forms which ask for names of referees can include a note such as: 'Your agreement may also be sought to reference inquiries being made of all previous employers and to the timing of any approach to your current employer.'

While it may be considered ethically unsound to conduct any reference inquiry without the candidate's permission, a candidate's refusal to agree to a reference being sought obviously raises questions that need to be addressed at the interview stage. It may therefore be best to ask for a blanket agreement from the candidate for any or all previous managers to be contacted, as such a request will quickly bring to light any problem areas.

Written references

A request in writing to a referee which merely states that the person concerned has applied for a particular post and says 'Your observations would be appreciated' (or words to that effect) rarely produces an illuminating reference. If no indications are given to the referee about the factors of most importance, the written response is likely to do little more than confirm the existence of the referee and his or her subjective and perhaps biased opinion of the candidate.

To ensure that written references produce useful information, referees must be pointed towards providing the relevant details being sought. This falls into two parts: confirmation of factual data, and more judgmental views. When writing to previous employers it is worth checking the information the candidate has supplied. For example, the letter seeking a reference can state:

> John Smith has given us the following information about his previous employment with your organisation. We would be grateful if you could confirm or correct this information regarding his period of employment, job title, final salary and reason for leaving.

The letter can then move to matters which are important in the job for which the candidate is applying, for example:

> While any comment you may care to make about Mr Smith will be appreciated, we should be particularly interested to have your views on the following points, which are of specific importance to the job for which he is applying:
>
> ▪ quality of relationships with customers

- willingness to work unsocial hours
- ability to work well without supervision, and
- attendance record.

Some employers send the referee a job description of the post applied for and ask whether, in the referee's opinion, the person concerned would be a suitable appointee. This is a very questionable practice. The referee is unlikely to know enough about the inquirer's organisation to make a sound judgement. It is the potential employer's role, not the referee's, to judge selection suitability.

Checking qualifications

Recruitment specialists who regularly check qualifications suggest that as many as one in eight candidates falsify the information they provide to some extent, even if only by exaggerating the class of their university degree. There are two reasons for checking qualifications. For some jobs, a qualification may be an essential criterion: more generally, even if the qualifications concerned are not of critical importance, any significant falsification must raise questions about the candidate's integrity or judgement.

Qualifications can be checked by direct inquiry, normally by letter, to the institution concerned, eg university or professional body, quoting the person's name, claimed qualification and the date on which it was awarded. It may also be necessary to check the academic or professional status of institutions that are claimed to have awarded qualifications but which are not generally known. There are a number of bogus organisations in and outside the UK which sell prestigiously titled awards that are wholly worthless.

Personal references

It is useful to have written references when these need to be issued to a selection panel and in circumstances where formal reference records are considered desirable. In many cases, however, the most useful form of referencing is the systematic interviewing of the referee, either on the telephone or by arranging a face-to-face meeting. Many referees are very cautious about expressing anything other than rather bland views in a letter to an inquirer with whom they have had no personal contact. In a conversation they will say much more, and particular points of interest can be pursued in a way which is quite impossible through correspondence. As with written inquiries, telephone referencing or interviewing needs to be planned and structured to ensure coverage of issues of specific relevance to the job in question.

In addition, there are two general but key questions which can be asked in almost every case, and which are far more likely to be answered fully in a conversation than by letter:

Would you re-employ this person if the opportunity arose?

A 'no' or heavily qualified response can then be followed up by a more probing question.

Do you know of any reason why we should not employ this person?

Again, an adverse or hesitant response may indicate the need for further inquiry.

Further information

ANDLER E. *The Complete Reference Checking Handbook.* New York, Amacom, 1998.

8 Induction programmes

Induction is something of a Cinderella activity in some personnel departments, where it is delegated to the most inexperienced personnel officer and allocated far fewer resources than other training functions. In some organisations, planned induction is non-existent: new employees are plunged into their jobs without preparation and are expected to become effective largely by their own efforts. The common and costly result of inadequate induction is high turnover among short-service employees.

Effective induction recognises that new employees need help in adjusting to their new jobs and organisational environments. The primary aim of an induction programme is to help new employees quickly become fully integrated members of their working groups and prevent a high incidence of early leavers.

In planning an induction programme, the main issues to consider are the use of individual and group training, what information to impart over what timescales, the duration, content and training methods of formal courses, and the induction roles of line-managers and personnel staff.

Before examining each of these issues in more detail, it is worth noting that the induction process is influenced by the impressions and information that recruits gain during selection. One reason for early resignation is disillusionment caused by the reality of the job falling short of the image created by the job advertisement and at interview. Recruitment and selection need to be thought of as preliminary stages in an effective induction programme.

Training options

Whether to plan induction on an individual or group basis may appear to be largely a matter of logistics. Where new employees are recruited in batches, it obviously makes sense to keep them together for the formal elements of an induction programme. Where they join singly, at least some aspects of induction have to be handled individually. In practice, however, all new employees require some individual attention, although some group activities are both practicable and useful even when new starters are few and far between.

With large recruit intakes, there is a danger of relying solely on highly structured induction courses and assuming that induction concludes with the end of the course. But however well-planned such a course may be, induction is eventually a matter of each individual adjusting to a specific work situation. The transition from a well-organised course to what might be a less well-ordered job environment may be more traumatic than starting employment directly in the job. So, even when employees are recruited in batches, their induction course needs to feed into a planned, on-the-job process of assisting each person adjust to the realities of the job.

Most organisations recruit singly and sporadically to fill individual vacancies as and when they occur. This may appear to rule out any group induction training. In practice this need not be so, and to rely entirely on individual action runs the risk of topics such as general company information never being given the attention they deserve.

A significant proportion of the information which any induction programme should impart does not need to be given right at the start of employment. Initial individual induction can deal with immediate and practical issues such as premises layout, time-recording and job safety: broader topics (eg company history, staff development schemes) can be covered by courses run, say, every three months for all employees who have joined in the previous quarter.

Phasing of information

Induction programmes are concerned mainly with imparting information. The new employee needs to know about conditions of employment, organisation structure, safety rules and a host of other matters. But there are severe limits on how much information anyone can absorb in a short period, particularly when – as on the first day at work – the employee is bound to be experiencing a degree of tension. So induction needs to be spread over a reasonable time period, not crammed into an over-intensive first day or two.

A new employee's first concern is with very basic matters, such as the immediate geography of the workplace, canteen arrangements, and introductions to working colleagues. The organisation, too, has immediate requirements – to ensure, for example, that the employee understands essential safety regulations and is documented for entry on to the payroll. Once matters of this kind have been dealt with, the employee's interest will expand beyond the immediate job, and the range of induction topics can be broadened.

It is helpful to produce a checklist which defines the topics to be covered and the appropriate stage for each within the programme. A summarised example is given at the end of this chapter.

Precise timing and the extent to which employees are brought together in groups (particularly for the later stages) depend on the numbers involved and whether employees from different occupational groups or status levels can be mixed. Multi-occupational induction can contribute to building a commonality of interest and attitude across the workforce, while mixing status levels will suit those organisations that have the objective of reducing status distinctions.

Duration and content

Administrative convenience may seem to point to the maximum use of short, intensive, off-the-job induction courses – getting induction over quickly by packing as much as possible into a short time period. However, people's ability to maintain attention while passively absorbing information is very limited. So information is best given in small, digestible portions. Six two-hour sessions (each with a refreshment break) spread over four to eight weeks can be far more effective than a continuous two-day course.

As to what topics should be included in a formal course, one answer is as few as possible if the intention is to rely mainly on the conventional sequence of talks to new staff by the personnel, operational, and safety managers. Some subjects, such as explanations of bonus and pension schemes, may have to be dealt with in this way, though the extensive use of good visual aids, supplemented by well-designed and clearly written handouts, is essential. But for other topics, factory visits, videos, and discussion groups are far more effective.

Safety, for example, can be dealt with in a dramatic manner by carefully planned demonstrations. The importance of customer relations can be effectively developed in a discussion group. Company activities can be shown through visits, supplemented by films and videos. Other topics are best dealt with individually, rather than in a course setting.

The manager's role

Effective induction requires the involvement both of line managers and personnel or training specialists. In highly formalised programmes, there is a danger of the trainers monopolising the process, and minimising the important role of the manager. This managerial role concentrates on the employee as an individual and has several aspects.

First, managers can introduce the new employees to their immediate supervisors who will in turn introduce them to their work colleagues. Secondly, managers and supervisors can ensure that adequate information is given about day-to-day matters such as time-recording, details of the pay system as they apply to a particular job, canteen breaks and on-site safety. The manager can also make the link for an employee between induction training and job training, and monitor the new recruit's progress, taking any necessary supportive action.

The employee's supervisor or manager may not need to handle all these matters personally but should ensure they are dealt with. One useful form of delegation is to designate a reliable and helpful existing employee as the starter's buddy, with a checklist of topics to explain – such as the geography of the plant.

The personnel manager's main roles are to design and monitor induction programmes, to handle personally some aspects (for example, to deal with first-day reception and documentation, to take some formal group sessions on, say, staff development or pension schemes), to provide a welfare and counselling service to new employees, and to help them overcome induction problems.

The personnel manager should also check that the induction programme meets the needs of several categories of employees whose special circumstances are often overlooked. These include existing staff who are being transferred or promoted and who can be consulted individually about the help they need in adjusting to their new jobs.

Another such group is part-timers, who are too often omitted from formal induction because courses are planned to fit only full-timers' hours of work. People with disabilities (who may have mobility problems with factory tours and lecture-room sessions) and ethnic minorities (particularly if they have language difficulties) may also need special attention.

In planning an induction programme, it is helpful to use a checklist of the topics to be covered, indicating who is responsible for each and the time period in which each should be completed. An example follows on page 61.

Topic	Who is responsible?			By when?		
	Personnel	Supervisor	Manager	1st day	1st week	1st month
1 Reception						
Documentation	X			X		
Intro. to supervisor	X			X		
2 Department						
Geography		X		X		
Organisation and function		X				X
3 The company						
Products			X	X		
Core values			X	X		
4 Employment terms						
Timekeeping	X			X		
Pay system		X			X	
Other terms	X				X	
5 Health and safety						
Immediate hazards		X			X	
Protective clothing		X			X	
6 Rules and procedures						
Conduct & discipline		X			X	
Grievances	X			X		
7 Communication/ consultation						
TU recognition	X				X	
Briefing groups		X				X
8 Performance						
Customer relations			X			X
Appraisals	X					X
9 Training and development	X					X
10 Benefits						
Staff restaurant	X			X		
Social club	X					X

Further reading

1 FOWLER A. *Employee Induction: A good start.* 3rd edn. London, Institute of Personnel and Development, 1996.
2 ACAS. *Induction of New Employees.* London, Advisory, Conciliation and Arbitration Service, 1985.

Signing them up

9   Employment contracts

Provisions on written statements of terms and conditions in the 1993 Trade Union Reform and Employment Rights Act – now incorporated in the 1998 Employment Rights Act – caused most employers to revise the documentation they used when making appointments. Growth in the use of fixed-term contracts, and the substitution of personal contracts for conditions determined by collective bargaining, have also focused attention on contract documents. Two commonly held beliefs about contracts cause confusion in reviews of employment documentation:

- the idea that an employment contract has to be a single, written document
- the notion that there is a legal requirement to issue all employees with such contracts.

Neither of these is true.

Under common law, a contract comes into existence when two parties reach an agreement which both intend should be legally binding. Contracts also come into existence when one party makes an offer, the other accepts it and the agreement is supported by 'consideration' (a legal term meaning something of value which passes from one party to the other). The salary forms the consideration in an employment contract. For a contract to exist, none of these elements need be in writing: an oral offer and acceptance suffice.

The misconception that there is a statutory requirement to issue employment contracts may originate with the 1963 Contracts of Employment Act, whose title appeared to support this view. This Act prescribed certain terms which had to be incorporated in contracts of employment (such as minimum notice periods) but did not require the production of written contracts as such.

The 1993 requirement to issue a detailed written statement of particulars does not imply that this statement is the contract. It is only evidence of what the employer considers are some of the contractual terms. If there is a legal dispute about a difference between the written statement and any contractual documents, then the terms in the contractual documents will prevail. Although the law does not require a contract document to be issued, it is a matter of good practice to specify the terms of the contract in writing and thus prevent any later misunderstandings about mutual rights and obligations.

At this point, the other common misconception occurs – that a written contract must be a single, legally drafted document, signed by both parties. It can be, but it may also take the form of an exchange of letters. The employer writes offering a job, giving some details about terms (generally salary). The employee writes back, accepting the offer. This written offer and acceptance, which includes the 'consideration' of salary, fully meets the requirement for a contract to come into existence, even if the word 'contract' is not used. Furthermore, a written acceptance by the employee is not essential, as the fact of starting work can be taken as implying acceptance of the employer's offer.

To prevent ambiguity about the terms of the contract, it is advisable to do more than rely simply on a short offer letter and its implied acceptance, though for the majority of a normal workforce there is no need to go as far as the issue and joint signing of a lengthy legal document. That type of document is generally reserved for use in senior management appointments, particularly when complex arrangements for share options or restrictive covenants need to be defined or the contract is for a fixed term. For most appointments, it is sufficient to write a letter offering the job and describing the terms. Two copies can be given to the employee, with the request:

Please sign and return one copy of this letter, retaining the other for your records.

I confirm my acceptance of the offer and terms set out above:

Signed ....

Date ....

To comply with the requirements for a written statement of terms, and to ensure that the contract and the statement are compatible, the offer letter can state:

The terms and conditions of your employment, in addition to those described in this letter, will be as set out in the attached statement, which is issued in accordance with the requirements of section 1 of the Employment Rights Act 1998.

This will incorporate the terms of the statement in the contract.

The Act does not require the statement to be issued with the offer, and allows for details of some of the terms to be issued in instalments during the first two months of employment. In almost all cases, however, it is better to issue the whole statement at one time, and combine its issue with the job offer. This may involve some duplication of details between the offer letter and the statement, particularly as the latter must now identify the parties and include such details as the date employment commences, remuneration and job title. The practical implication is for fairly brief offer letters, leaving most of the detail to the written statement. The repetition of job title, salary and start date in the offer letter should not be a problem, although the statement will need to be revised if events cause the actual start date to differ from that originally offered and accepted.

For organisations with devolved units or subsidiary companies, it is particularly important that the documentation identifies the employer. Is it the group or parent company, or the subsidiary? Problems about job transfers or liability for redundancy payments may arise if the identity of the employer is unclear.

The Act permits the use of a brief job description as an alternative to a job title. In most cases, this is best avoided in order to prevent the description being incorporated into the contract and thus inhibiting later job flexibility. If a separate job description is issued with the offer letter, it is advisable for it to include a statement to the effect:

> This job description is a guide to the work you will initially be required to undertake. It may be changed from time to time to meet changing circumstances. It does not form part of your contract of employment.

Even the most comprehensive documentation need not include all the terms which the law will read into a contract. There are four types of contractual terms: express terms, implied terms, incorporated terms and statutory terms.

1 Express terms: those that are specified, either in writing or by oral agreement

2 Implied terms are those so obvious that they do not need to be specified – particularly the obligation that the employer and employee must behave in a way that preserves mutual trust and confidence

3 Incorporated terms are most commonly the terms of collective agreements for those employees whose pay and conditions are determined by collective bargaining. These are incorporated into individual contracts by a statement to that effect – for example:

> Your terms and conditions of employment are as set out in the agreement between the organisa- tion and the . . . trade union . . . as amended from time to time.

This clause may need to refer to both national and local agreements, and should be specific, both as to the agreements concerned and to the fact that future changes to these agreements will be incorporated in the individual contracts. The Employment Rights Act also requires a number of the terms in incorporated agreements (such as holidays and hours of work) to be described in the written statement of particulars

4   Statutory terms are those which various statutes require to be included in all employment contracts, or are implied by statute to apply, whether or not the contract documents mention them. Examples include minimum notice periods, equal pay rights, and employees' rights under the Wages Act.

There are circumstances for which specific contract clauses are needed. For example, a fixed-term contract must specify its duration and termination date. Non-renewal of a fixed-term contract normally constitutes dismissal. To avoid unfair dismissal or redundancy claims, it is necessary to include an agreed waiver clause and to require the employee to provide a signed acceptance. Waiver clauses for unfair dismissal can be included in fixed-term contracts of one year or more: redundancy waivers can be included only in contracts with two years or more duration. A clause is needed to the effect:

In accordance with Section 197 of the Employment Rights Act 1998, the employee agrees to waive the right to a redundancy payment or to make a complaint of unfair dismissal on the expiry and non-renewal of this contract.

A contract may also be needed for the duration of a particular project, or only until a certain event occurs, without the date of the event or project completion being known. To avoid unfair dismissal or redundancy claims, a clause is needed which defines the circumstances that will terminate the contract; for example:

> This contract will terminate on the date on which the firm's computer facility is transferred to Basingstoke.

Mobility clauses can prevent contractual difficulties when an employee is required to transfer to a different job or location. A typical clause might read:

> You may be required to transfer to such other work as the company may reasonably require from time to time and to any of the company's departments or work locations.

Any other statements in the contract documentation about the job on offer and its location must be compatible with this clause – for example, by stating in the offer letter that the employee will initially be employed in the stated location. It must be noted, however, that the courts are unlikely to uphold mobility clauses which are unreasonable in the light of an employee's individual circumstances.

Contracts of employees in senior posts or those working on highly confidential matters may need to include clauses which specifically bar them from revealing trade secrets. An example of such clause follows:

> Except in the proper discharge of your duties under the contract, you will not, during or after the termination of your employment, disclose to any person or organisation any information which comes into your possession relating to the company, its business or customers, without

first obtaining the permission of the company, organisation or person concerned.

Clauses can also be included which prevent the employees working for competitors or soliciting their employers' customers for a set period after they leave the organisation's employment. The case law relating to these restrictive covenants is very complex, as the courts are reluctant to enforce restrictions on personal freedom. This is an aspect of contract documentation on which personnel managers are well advised to seek expert legal advice.

Further information

1 AIKIN O. *Contracts*. 2nd edn. London, Institute of Personnel and Development, 1997.

2 IDS. *Contracts of Employment*. Employment Law Handbook, series 2, no. 15. London, Incomes Data Services, 1998.

10   Fixed-term contracts

Fixed-term contracts are often thought of only as complex legal documents setting out the employment terms of company directors. What is not always realised is that legally, a fixed-term contract is simply one which runs for a set period of time, regardless of the precise form of its documentation, or whether there is any documentation at all. A part-time cleaner who orally accepts employment for a defined three-month period is just as much on a fixed-term contract as the chief executive with an eight-page document defining the terms of a three-year rolling contract. There are several reasons for the use of fixed-term contracts:

- to retain an employee for a known, required period
- to prevent a key employee leaving at an inconvenient time
- to create an opportunity to review and if necessary terminate employment without incurring legal liabilities
- to motivate an employee (usually a senior manager) to produce results within a defined period

to attract an employee who wishes to have a secure but not indefinite period of employment.

The basic principle at common law is that if both parties to a contract agree that it will start and end on predetermined dates, its termination on the expiry date does not constitute a dismissal. Examples of relevant fixed-term contract clauses are:

This contract will terminate on 31 March 2002.

The contract will run for three years from 1 July 1999.

A variant to which similar common law principles apply is known as a performance or task contract. In this case, the parties agree the contract will terminate on the completion of a task, or when specific circumstances occur, even though the date of termination cannot be specified in advance. Specimen clauses are:

The contract will terminate on the date on which the project completion certificate is signed.

The contract is for the duration of the programme and will end when the budgeted funds for the programme are exhausted.

In both fixed-term and performance contracts, wrongful termination during the period of the contract gives rise to a liability for damages for breach of contract. This normally amounts to the value of benefits for the unexpired period of the contract, though with a possible deduction for the monies the employee might reasonably have been expected to earn after finding alternative employment (ie mitigation of loss).

However, the Employment Rights Act 1998 overrides

the common law position so far as unfair dismissal and redundancy are concerned, though only for fixed-term, not performance, contracts. Under the Act, the expiry and non-renewal of a contract which has a defined termination date does constitute a dismissal. Potentially, this gives rise to unfair dismissal and redundancy rights – except where certain exclusions apply. It does not mean that non-renewal is inherently unfair – only that if the decision not to renew is unreasonable (using the same criteria as for any unfair dismissal case) the employee has the right of access to an Employment Tribunal. The most likely cause of an unfair non-renewal is for the employer not to offer this when there is still a requirement for someone to undertake the same work, or suitable alternative work is available. This amounts to unfair redundancy.

It is possible (and common practice) to escape from these risks of legal action by the use of waiver clauses. Unfair dismissal rights are excluded when the contract is for a fixed term of one year or more, the dismissal consists only of non-renewal, and the employee has agreed to the exclusion of these rights in writing before the contract expiry date. The exclusion of redundancy rights is as for unfair dismissal, except that the contract must be for two years or more.[1] To take advantage of these exclusions, it is necessary to include an agreed waiver within the contract documentation. An example is:

> The employee agrees to waive any unfair dismissal and redundancy rights which may otherwise arise on the expiry and non-renewal of this contract.

No waiver clauses are needed in performance contracts,

as unfair dismissal and redundancy rights do not accrue on their expiry – provided there is no ambiguity about their status.

Problems about the application of waiver clauses can arise when fixed-term contracts are renewed or extended. The difference between renewals and extensions of contracts is important. Extensions are often arranged informally, and for quite short periods. The employee may simply be asked to stay on for a few days or weeks, with both parties assuming the contract continues. In these cases – or even when the extension is confirmed in writing – 1998 case law indicates that the waiver clauses in the basic contracts carries forward into the extension period, even though this period may be less than a year. However, if a contract is renewed as distinct from extended, and particularly if some of the terms of the original contract are changed, the courts will probably interpret the renewed contract as a new contract which needs its own waiver clause – provided the contract period is for at least one year (for waiving unfair dismissal rights) or two years (for redundancy rights). An alternative may be possible – to define the extension as a new performance contract which will expire when a particular task has been completed.

There has been significant criticism of the use of waiver clauses as giving employers too easy a way of depriving employees of the protection of unfair dismissal and redundancy legislation. In mid-1998, the government sought views on this issue in the context of consultation about its 'Fairness at Work' white paper.

Whether or not a waiver clause is used, it is helpful for both parties if a clause is included which recognises that a decision about renewal is best made some time before the contract's expiry date. A typical clause is:

A decision as to whether a renewal of this contract will be offered will be made not later than [date].

There are two issues relating to very short fixed-term contracts of the type for which detailed contract documents are rarely used. If a person is engaged on a contract for one month or less, but through renewals stays in employment for three months or more, they acquire the same rights to statutory notice periods as employees on contracts of indefinite duration. Employees engaged on fixed-term contracts for three months or less, or on performance contracts which are not expected to last for three months, are not entitled to guarantee payments, statutory sick pay or medical suspension pay – unless, by extensions, they work for more than three months.

A waiver clause applies only to the termination and non-renewal of a contract at its designated expiry date. Dismissals during the life of a fixed-term contract are subject to the same redundancy and unfair dismissal provisions as apply to employees generally, provided, of course, that the appropriate length of service has been achieved. These provisions also apply if the non-renewal is for reasons other than the simple expiry of the contract. Thus, if an employee is told the contract is not being renewed because of dissatisfaction with conduct or performance, there may be a potential action for unfair dismissal. Contracts are often not renewed simply because there is no longer any requirement for an employee to do the work involved. When no waiver clause exists, this creates a potential redundancy. This does not mean that such redundancy is unfair – only that the employee (if he or she has two years or more continuous employment) has a right to be consulted, to be considered fairly for other work, and to a redundancy payment.

It is recommended good practice for the employer to make clear that the contract may be terminated at any time if the employee is in serious breach of contract. A typical termination clause to cover this eventuality follows:

> The employer may terminate this contract at any time if the employee:
> - commits gross misconduct or is in serious neglect of duty
> - wilfully fails to abide by the company's policies or procedures
> - breaches the duties of fidelity and confidentiality
> - brings the company into disrepute
> - is unable through illness or accident to perform the contractual duties either permanently or for a period exceeding six months.

It is less common to include any provision for the employee to terminate the contract, although some public sector contracts include a clause stating that termination, other than by expiry, shall be by three months notice on either side. While such a clause introduces greater flexibility for both employer and employee, it partially destroys the fixed-term nature of the contract by taking away the guarantee – for both employer and employee – of employment for the whole of the fixed term.

A clause for termination by notice is clearly necessary

in a rolling contract. This is a contract, commonly for three years, which is automatically renewed on a set date each year – typically on 1 January or the beginning of the company's financial year. Unless there is a clause in the contract by which either party can give designated notice to prevent the automatic rollover, the contract will continue indefinitely. Rolling contracts, particularly those without notice clauses, have been criticised for the very high costs involved in their termination. In effect, they provide a three-year notice period with the possibility of the employer having to pay upwards of three years' salary if the contract is terminated. If they are used at all, they need a clause stating that either party may give notice (say, six months) that they do not wish this renewal to occur.

Further reading

1 AIKIN O. *Contracts*. 2nd edn. London, Institute of Personnel and Development, 1997.
2 IDS. *Contracts of Employment*. Employment Law Handbook, series 2, no. 15. London, Incomes Data Services, 1998.

End-note

1 The present Labour Government has suggested reducing this to one year in its 'Fairness at Work' white paper.

11 Annual hours contracts

A major theme of current people management is the emphasis on the need for flexibility in the way people are employed and in the way work is organised. Employment costs have come under increasingly close scrutiny, with particular attention being given to ways of reducing levels of expensive, premium-rated overtime and shift work. One result has been a greater use of forms of employment other than conventional full-time jobs, and a consequent increase in the use of part-time, seasonal, temporary and fixed-term contracts. The other major development has been the introduction of annual hours systems.

The annual hours idea is simple in principle. Instead of employees working to a standard schedule of weekly hours, they are contracted to work a specified total number of hours within a 12-month period. The hours actually worked each week can then fluctuate to reflect changes in operational requirements of the organisation, so the conventional distinction between basic hours and overtime is eliminated. Pay administration is also simplified, as employees are paid the same weekly or monthly sum throughout the year, regardless of the precise number of hours they work each week.

Annual hours systems can be applied to almost any type of employment, although the benefits are less obvious in some situations than others. For example, if the work activity level remains constant throughout the year and does not require employees' attendance outside conventional weekday hours, annual hours contracts may have little advantage to offer.

The circumstances in which a wide variety of organisations have found significant benefit from annual hours include:

- fluctuating workloads, in which periods of intense activity, previously involving large overtime payments, are followed by slack episodes in which employees have had to be paid full wages for less than fully productive working time. With annual hours, the length of the working week can be varied to match operational requirements without the need for overtime payments in busy periods.
- work with a significant seasonal pattern, such as grounds maintenance, with a light workload in the winter and long hours needed in the summer; and factories producing goods which have seasonal sales peaks
- rostered shift-working, particularly when this has to include nights and weekends. Annual hours provide more flexibility in scheduling rest periods and holidays, as well as including a time allowance for covering sickness absence. Examples include process industries and leisure centres.

■ work which has unpredictable and often short-notice demand patterns – such as on-call service work and television production.

Although the principle is simple, designing an annual hours system can be complicated, and there is no one standard pattern. Employers need to consider the notional standard working day and week; whether all or some annual holiday hours are to be included; whether public holiday hours are to be included; whether to include additional 'bank hours' (eg for absence cover); and whether to designate 'reserve hours', such as for training time.

Annual hours totals have to be calculated on the basis of the hours in what would otherwise be the standard working week and day. In a survey of annual hours systems conducted by Incomes Data Services, the equivalent basic weekly hours across a variety of organisations ranged from 35 (in a building society) to 39 (with a process company), with a median of 37.5 giving a 7.5 hours basic day. Several organisations operate more than one annual hours schedule, with different annual totals either for different categories of employees, or to provide several options from which individual employees can choose. In the building society, for example, there were four options calculated on basic weekly hours of 35, 42, 45 or 48 – with different salaries to match. The concept here is to enable employees to choose, within limits, what total hours they wish to commit themselves to and, of course, be paid for.

Organisations are almost equally divided between those which include holidays in the annual hours total and those which keep holidays as a separately managed system. One reason for excluding holiday hours is when there is a fixed holiday shutdown. If no employees are to be at work for a scheduled period each year, that period can be excluded from the annual hours total because it is not a time when any flexibility in working arrangements is required. An example of how annual hours can be calculated is:

Basic 5-day weekly hours:	37.5
Basic daily hours:	7.5
Gross annual hours (260 × 7.5):	1,950.0
Less:	
8 public holidays:	−60.0
5 days end-year shut-down:	−37.5
Plus:	
7 bank days:	+52.5
Gross basic annual hours	1,905.0
of which 20 days are leave:	−150.0
Net annual hours:	1,755.0

If employees are allowed considerable freedom of choice in taking leave, there may be advantages in including holiday entitlements in the total. The annual hours then cover all paid time, not just working time. Consideration then needs to be given to how holiday absence is to be monitored, and whether it is acceptable for employees to take less leave than the amount built into the annual hours total. Another option is to exclude fixed holiday hours (eg for a Christmas to New Year shutdown) but include the balance of annual leave.

The position regarding public holidays may be influenced by whether or not any employees are required to work on those days, and if so, whether there is a continued entitlement to compensatory time off. If an organisation closes down for public holidays there is little point in including these hours in the annual total.

Bank hours may be added to the basic annual total to provide for some degree of additional unscheduled working – most commonly for absence cover. Some firms operating rostered shift-working add additional unrostered hours for this purpose. A paper mill, for example, operates a basic annual hours total calculated on a requirement to work 213 rostered shifts a year. To this is then added a requirement to be available to work hours equivalent to an additional 4.5 unrostered shifts to cover for absences.

Reserve hours are hours designated for specific purposes other than normal working, the most common of which is training. The amount depends on the company's training policy and may also vary between different categories of staff. One chemical company designates 72 hours a year as its training reserve for process technicians – equivalent to 10 working days based on a standard 36-hour week. In the IDS survey, the total of banked or reserve hours varied between organisations from 16 to 204.

At its simplest, pay for an annual hours contract is the annual value of what has previously been the basic weekly wage, paid in equal instalments throughout the year. There are, however, several options to consider.

Many organisations have introduced annual hours as one element in a major package of changes, including reductions in the standard working week and the introduction of new pay structures or shift systems (such as five-crew working). In these circumstances, the annual pay for new annual hours may be a figure (negotiated or decided) not based precisely on any previous hourly or weekly wage rate. With the elimination of variations in weekly pay caused by shift allowances and overtime payments, it may also be practicable to use annual hours to implement monthly cash-less pay in place of previous weekly cash wages. The element of the annual sum that should be calculated for bank or reserve hours needs careful consideration, as it is normal to pay for these hours, whether or not they are actually worked.

Finally, it may still be necessary to have an arrangement in place for paying overtime, if hours are worked beyond the annual hours total. This may involve a single annual payment for any such excess hours, as the annual total of hours actually worked will not be known until the end of the year.

While greater flexibility and the reduction, if not elimination, of overtime are obvious and major benefits, there are some potential difficulties in the operation of annual hours. One concerns employee stability. In an ideal annual hours system, all employees would each work a full 12 months so that short and long working periods are balanced to produce the targeted working total. But if labour turnover is high, employees starting and leaving during slack periods will have been paid for a higher average of weekly hours than they have actually worked. On a wider basis, it may also be necessary to retain separate arrangements for short-time working or lay-offs, to cope with unexpectedly large reductions in activity levels.

Annual hours are sometimes introduced to enable the

employer to call in employees at very short notice to meet unpredictable work peaks, or for other circumstances in which employees' working hours are subject to unrostered variation. In such cases, employees with domestic responsibilities may find it all but impossible to vary their child-minding arrangements as quickly as the changes that occur in work requirements. There may also be resistance to the introduction of annual hours from employees who have regularly earned large amounts of overtime, if this results in a significant cut in earnings. Offsetting this, however, are the benefits of guaranteed and stable level of earnings and some increase in leisure time.

Although standard holiday entitlement can be either included in the annual hours total or dealt with separately, problems can arise within annual hours about the treatment of other absences – particularly compassionate leave and occasional days of uncertificated sick leave. To what extent should such absences be credited as working time? Annual hours systems need to be paralleled by effective systems of absence management.

Finally, some organisations may be inhibited by the more complex administration required to keep track of each employee's attendance times. Difficulties can arise, too, when an employee in a rostered shift system changes shift crews within the year or transfers to a non-shift job. There are also many companies that employ white-collar staff with no form of time recording, and they may not wish to introduce the more detailed attendance controls needed for accurate monitoring of annual hours contracts.

Further information

1 IDS. *Annual Hours.* IDS Study No. 544. London, Incomes Data Services, 1993.

2 HUTCHINSON S. *Annual Hours Working in the UK.* IPD research paper. London, Institute of Personnel Management, 1993.

12 Managing expatriates

Expatriate management was for many years concerned primarily with employment in ex-colonial countries. This gave rise to a concept of the expatriate as an adventurer; living with risks, especially to health, but enjoying a far higher standard of living than could ever have been achieved at home. Oil exploration and civil engineering, particularly in the Middle East, carried this concept into more recent decades. Today, not least as a result of closer European involvement, the expatriate is more likely to be office based and working in an economy which may well have higher living standards than the UK.

Another change concerns language skills. The traditional UK expatriate could operate successfully for years without picking up more than a smattering of local languages. It was accepted, by expatriate and indigenous employees alike, that English was the language of industrial and commercial management. Now, in countries such as France, Germany or Japan, expatriates need to acquire new language skills rapidly, something which puts them at an initial disadvantage compared with the often greater linguistic abilities of their foreign colleagues.

In addition to recognising and, perhaps, correcting the expectations of potential expatriates and dealing with the language issue, organisations with no experience in expatriate management need to realise the considerable additional costs involved. The total benefits package is likely to be pitched at a higher level than for a comparable UK post, and the cost of failure can also be very high, in terms of both reputation and replacement. So, before arranging an overseas posting, the first question to address is whether a local appointment is a practicable alternative. Advice about the availability of local candidates, and the methods and costs of recruitment and selection, can usually be obtained from the UK-based trade sections of foreign embassies, from home and overseas employers' organisations, and from the relevant government departments in the country concerned.

If there is no local alternative, the matters to consider can be grouped under the headings of suitability and selection; training and career planning; conditions of service; remuneration; and monitoring and counselling.

Suitability and selection

Although most of the selection criteria for any particular appointment will be specific to the job and the country, there are important characteristics that apply in all cases. A starting point is to recognise that high performance in a UK setting is not a guarantee of success in an overseas posting. Too little consideration to the impact on the individual of differences in the business, social and cultural environment has often led to the failure of an expatriate who is technically excellent but psychologically unsuited.

Any overseas posting involves a period of personal adjustment to cultural change. Qualities such as adaptability, stress resistance and empathy are of much greater importance than may be evident in a normal UK setting. A lively interest in the historical, environmental or political background of the country concerned is another positive attribute. Thorough, structured interviewing to probe these factors is essential – even of existing employees whom the organisation may feel it knows well already. Personality characteristics can be investigated by appropriate psychometric tests. There are some personality inventories designed specifically for expatriate selection: advice is available from other major test producers about the qualities to test for, and the best general tests to use.

Personal and family circumstances are also a major influence, and these need to be discussed openly with the potential expatriate. The three main issues are:

- the partner's attitude to the move. It can be helpful for selectors to meet this person to explain and discuss the implications of the posting.
- children's education. Arrangements may be needed to assist the employee, whether the children are to go to school in the UK, or to be educated abroad.
- housing. Employers may need to offer assistance or advice about retaining ownership of a UK property and letting it for the period of overseas service.

Training and career planning

Ideally, the employer and employee should see an overseas posting as an element in a long-term career development plan. The opportunities it provides to broaden experience and develop new skills should be identified and discussed, together with some indication of the probable career route to be followed on re-entry to the UK. There is often reluctance to accept an overseas posting for fear of missing UK promotion opportunities, and this needs to be addressed positively. It may be necessary to provide reassurances that, in the event of unexpected career opportunities occurring during the period abroad, the expatriate will be given equal consideration with UK-based colleagues.

In addition to this general scene-setting, any UK employee who has not worked in the country concerned needs specific briefing about every aspect of the planned move. This may include information about the relevant overseas company procedures and personalities but, in all cases, briefing about the country's culture is needed. Companies should be cautious about leaving this briefing to managers with extensive personal experience, as they are not always sufficiently sensitive to the factors (some of which may, with hindsight, seem trivial) which cause newcomers the most concern. There are a number of organisations offering specialist expatriate briefing courses, and most of these encourage the involvement of spouses – a practice certainly to be recommended.

Language training is an even more specific requirement in an increasing number of cases. Many people find that a mixture of course attendance and distance learning is the most effective method, and a range of courses and learning packages are on offer from specialist training providers. Too much reliance should not be placed on popularised self-teaching packages, which tend towards over-optimism in their claims about the time taken to learn to converse fluently.

Conditions of service

In designing the employment package, there are many issues to consider in addition to remuneration. The most important are:

- medical clearance and general health advice, particularly for work in the Third World or elsewhere where medical facilities are poor
- health and accident insurance – a guarantee of airlifting back to the UK in serious cases will do much to ease underlying worries
- educational provision – possibly through payment or subsidy of school fees in the UK or abroad
- overseas housing and furnishing arrangements
- clothing allowances for work in the tropics
- shipping and insurance of personal effects
- advice or assistance over shipping of pets and quarantine arrangements
- leave: the duration of local and home leave, the extent to which costs of family travel are met, the class of travel, and so on.

There is also the overriding question of the duration of the posting. Should this be for a defined term, or open-ended? Traditionally, the two- or three-year tour of duty has been very common, followed by as much as three months home leave if UK visits have not been possible during the period abroad. This type of arrangement is not so relevant for work in other countries within Europe, where weekends in the UK are entirely practicable and the climate is not a factor. For the purposes of career planning, however, a reasonably firm duration is generally preferable to a wholly open-ended arrangement.

Remuneration

The most complex single issue in expatriate management is remuneration. Designing the right payments package is influenced by:

- exchange rates
- taxation and social security costs
- differences in living costs
- differences in comparative salary levels
- possible restrictions on home remittances
- the expatriate's expectations
- the attitudes or reactions of local staff.

The importance of obtaining expert advice on such issues – particularly on UK and overseas taxation – cannot be over-emphasised. There may be significant tax advantages for both the employee and the company if a particular type of remuneration package is evolved; conversely, even an apparently minor feature can lead to a heavy tax burden. All these matters differ widely from country to country. Here it is only possible to highlight the main issues. There are several variants in payments policies:

- the home-based system: using UK salary structures for basic pay plus overseas allowances if appropriate

- the host-based system: paying the expatriate on local pay scales, possibly with expense payments to compensate for specific additional costs related to working overseas
- a unified salary system: using a common salary structure for UK and overseas operations, though probably with adjustments to reflect major differences in tax and social security costs.

The choice of system needs to take account of attitudes and expectations, as well as financial technicalities. It is normal for employees being posted abroad to expect some financial gain as an incentive, or as compensation for the domestic upheaval involved. As Europe becomes more integrated and the interchange of European nationals grows, the justification for financial inducements to accept overseas postings will be reduced. Technically, the term 'expatriate in Europe' has not been appropriate since 1992. In practical terms, however, this expectation of financial benefit remains a significant influence. The attitude of local employees also needs to be considered. Their ready acceptance of a foreign colleague will be inhibited by any perception that the expatriate is unjustifiably higher paid, a factor which may be in direct conflict with the expatriate's own expectations.

Monitoring

The success of an overseas posting can depend critically on skilful monitoring of an expatriate's integration and performance and on the availability of sensitive counselling before major difficulties occur. Expatriates often experience a stage of depression after an initial period of enthusiasm and interest and at this low point feel very isolated. Several measures can help to avoid this becoming a serious problem. A colleague in the UK can be nominated as the expatriate's personal mentor – a contact to telephone and be telephoned by at any time on any issue.

Every effort can also be made to keep the expatriate in touch with UK activities – through company journals, being kept on the circulation list for memos and notices (even if they have no relevance to the overseas situation), and special newsletters. It also helps if the expatriate can be flown home for important meetings or company events. Finally, expatriates should be visited as frequently as possible by relevant UK staff and have the chance of an appraisal and counselling discussion, preferably more than once a year.

Further information

1 The IPD's *European Management Guides,* researched and written by the international department of Incomes Data Services, particularly those dealing with recruitment, pay, and terms and conditions. The three titles are:
Contracts and Terms and Conditions of Employment. Incomes Data Services. London, Institute of Personnel and Development, 1994; *Industrial Relations and Collective Bargaining.* Ditto, 1996; *Recruitment, Training and Development.* Ditto, 1997.

2 BARON A. *and* WALTERS M. *The Culture Factor.* London, Institute of Personnel and Development, 1994.

3 HOGG C. *The Expatriate Manager.* London, Kluwer Publishing, 1988.

Putting them on the payroll

13   Salary surveys

There are several reasons why information about other employers' salary levels is valuable. An adverse trend in staff turnover may be related to pay falling behind market trends; it could help to identify appropriate pay rates when recruiting staff to new types of job; or a trade union may be pressing for pay rises by quoting higher salaries allegedly offered by other employers. More generally, organisations need to be aware of comparative salary levels, particularly if they have a policy of maintaining pay at a set relationship to the market and retaining a reputation as good employers.

There is a range of proprietary sources of salary data. Some are available only to subscribing organisations participating in surveys run by specialist consultancies. Others, such as the government's annual New Earnings Survey, are published. Such sources can help to monitor salary levels and trends, but their wide coverage often makes it difficult to match jobs precisely.

More focused salary data may be obtained through membership of a salary survey 'club' – a group of companies that have agreed to exchange information on a regular basis. If no such club exists, it might be worth approaching relevant organisations and suggesting one, although the initiating party is likely to be expected to handle all the administration of such a scheme. The format of this kind of club's salary survey may have to be a compromise to meet the different needs of its members, and it may therefore not meet the full requirements of any one organisation. If suitable data cannot be obtained from any published, subscribed or club surveys, a tailor-made approach is necessary. This applies particularly when very specific information is needed, such as sales commission formulae and pay levels in a defined commercial sector.

The first step is to decide precisely what information is required, bearing in mind that the response rate to an inquiry on one or two topics is likely to be far better than if respondents are asked to complete a long and complex questionnaire. It is tempting to add questions to a survey on the grounds that the resultant information might be interesting. For example, when researching the starting salary of newly qualified accountants, a finance director may suggest asking about pay of accountancy technicians or the numbers of accountants holding different qualifications. The risk of a more complicated survey inducing a poor response to the key question must then be set against the possible benefits of a wider range of information.

One of the principal issues in any survey is to decide how to ensure an acceptable level of data comparability. Both the organisations and the jobs must be matched carefully. When selecting participants, it is important to be aware that variations in company size and sector could make a significant difference to pay levels and practices. Senior management salaries, for instance, are strongly influenced by company size. So a survey in this field should either be restricted to organisations of a similar size or should also ask for basic data about, say, annual financial turnover or the size of the workforce, so that the scale can be identified.

Salary levels or related issues, such as the use of bonus or commission payments, may also differ between industries or sectors. If the aim is to study the pay of directly comparable jobs in directly comparable organisations, participation will need to be restricted to companies known to be of similar size in the same sector, perhaps even in the same region. If there is a concern about losing staff to different types of organisation or different sectors, or if information is needed in order to recruit from new sources, the survey will need to cast its net more widely.

Ensuring an acceptable match of jobs usually requires a compromise between complete accuracy and generalisations. There are very few jobs that are precisely the same in different organisations. A variety of work systems and supervisory arrangements may exist, even in jobs that appear, superficially, to be identical. Job titles can be particularly misleading. If the survey asks for salary data against its own detailed job descriptions, it may well be told that no such jobs exist elsewhere. A normal and more satisfactory approach is to prepare simple profiles that are based on real jobs but allow some flexibility. Participants should be able to match this profile with their own specific jobs, and they can then be asked to give salary details. An example of such a profile follows:

- job: training officer or equivalent title
- organisational context: an organisation with a

service bias, private or public sector, with a
workforce of between 500 and 1500

- reports to: head of personnel, or head of training if
  this is a separate function
- duties: prepares and delivers training material
  within topic areas and policies specified by or
  agreed with his/her manager. Discusses training
  needs with users and undertakes training needs
  analyses. Topic areas generally restricted to people
  management and organisational skills. Tutoring
  mainly at supervisory and lower management
  levels.
- experience: likely to be a graduate with at least
  three years' personnel or line management
  experience.

It may help to add two boxes to the questionnaire. In
one, respondents can indicate if the job they are matching is the same, or whether it is at a slightly higher or
lower level of responsibility than that of the profile. In
the other, they can show whether they are giving details
of an actual job, or quoting the salary they would pay if
they had a job of this kind.

The next step is to decide what precise salary information to request, and in what form. Terminology is
important, as a question asking simply for 'current salary'
may be interpreted in different ways by different respondents. Some may restrict their replies to basic salary and
omit bonuses or individual performance payments.
Others may quote pay ranges or grades, rather than actual
salaries. If a picture of the complete remuneration package is needed, the survey must ask for data about each

job under headings such as basic salary; additional payments included in monthly salary (performance pay, sales commission); and any additional periodic payments (annual profit or merit bonuses). A simpler approach is to ask for basic pay and total cash remuneration. Where pay varies, the questionnaire should ask for averages over a set period.

The survey also needs to be clear about whether it is asking for details of actual salaries, as paid to current jobholders, or details of the salary grades or scales appropriate to each job. Each approach has its disadvantages. If a respondent organisation has a number of employees in one of the surveyed jobs, but has no formal pay scales or uses broad pay bands, a request for actual salaries may be answered with an average of actual salaries, the midpoint of the scale, or even a comment that there are too many employees on too many different salaries to provide data.

A request simply for pay-scale data (minimum and maximum pay for each job) may be easier for a respondent to answer, but may not give a true picture. This is particularly the case if the pay scales are wide. The current trend towards broadbanding is resulting in pay scales with maxima as much as 75 per cent above their minima. So, a reply that the scale for a particular job is, say, £20,000–£35,000 is unlikely to contribute much to a comparison of actual pay levels. It may be that most of the company's employees are paid the maximum for their grade but, equally, it may be only a few top performers who ever progress to the upper part of the scale.

For these reasons, some surveys ask for both actual salaries (averages if several employees earn different amounts for similar jobs) and salary scales -although this can make the questionnaire rather complex. The more specific the request for information, the more likely it is to obtain a useful response.

To encourage replies, it is advisable to guarantee confidentiality. It can also be helpful to telephone potential survey targets in advance, partly to discover whether they are likely to participate, and partly to check what type of salary inquiry they would respond to most easily and find most useful. Data collection should always be by questionnaire in, as far as possible, a multiple-choice, rather than a narrative, format. It is common courtesy to supply prepaid envelopes for replies.

Further information

1 ARMSTRONG M. *Employee Reward.* London, Institute of Personnel and Development, 1996.
2 IDS. *Directory of Salary Surveys.* London, Incomes Data Services, updated annually.

14   Job evaluation schemes

Job evaluation, once a highly regarded management tool, has come under fire in recent times. Its critics say that because it assesses the job, rather than the job-holder, it fails to recognise the contribution of the individual. It has also been argued that the detailed job descriptions involved in some schemes serve to inhibit flexibility.

Yet research by the IPD and ACAS has indicated that the use of job evaluation has been on the increase. There are probably three reasons for this trend: the legal requirement for 'equal pay for work of equal value'; the need for new job evaluation schemes to support simpler pay structures; and the introduction of competency-based job evaluation.

Selecting the right job evaluation system is crucial if the resulting pay framework is to be consistent with an organisation's structure, style and values. But there is no single best scheme. Each organisation needs to assess its own requirements and set these against the range of available methods. The various types of job evaluation can be grouped into two broad categories:

- non-analytical methods, which assess each job as a whole
- analytical methods, which score each job against a number of factors.

Examples of the first type include whole-job ranking, where jobs are compared with each other and placed in rank order; paired comparisons, where each job is compared with every other job and assessed as bigger, the same or smaller; job classification, where each job is placed in a category defined by a standardised job description; and market comparisons, where jobs are matched against standard job descriptions for which market data are available.

The analytical methods all involve some form of points-scoring, based either on job factors (such as responsibility and complexity) or on competencies (including, for example, communication skills and leadership). In some schemes, every job is evaluated and scored; in others, only benchmark jobs are evaluated fully and other positions are compared and slotted in against the benchmarks. This type of system is often described as factor comparison. It is usually deployed when very large numbers of jobs are involved.

There are other choices to make, which concern the administration of the scheme and whether to use a proprietary procedure or to design a bespoke system. Administrative decisions include whether to use a computer-assisted method, whether to involve employee representatives and whether to operate an appeals process. The use of competencies also involves choices.

Competencies may be either specific to each kind of job, or generic – those that apply to all jobs.

The choice of a job evaluation scheme needs to be determined primarily by setting the characteristics of different methods against the organisation's circumstances and objectives. The main questions to address are as follows:

- Is the principal aim to meet the requirements of equal pay legislation? If the answer is yes, then all the non-analytical, whole-job methods must be ruled out. The 1983 equal value amendment to the Equal Pay Act 1970 states that pay rates must be the same when work is of equal value in terms of the demands made on a worker under various headings – for instance, effort, skill, decision. This implies that job-sizing must assess jobs on an analytical, factor-by-factor, not whole job, basis. There is no legal requirement for these factors to be the three quoted in the amendment because these are simply examples, but it is important to use clearly defined factors that are free of any direct or indirect sexual bias. The safest factors are those that are impersonal and wholly job-related, such as responsibility for resources or task complexity. If competency factors are used, they too need to be defined carefully to avoid any implication of indirect sexual stereotyping
- How many different jobs are to be evaluated? Apart from the equal pay issue, most whole-job methods are suitable only if a relatively small number of jobs are involved, otherwise they become unwieldy.

For example, in the paired comparison method, the evaluation of 50 jobs would require 1,225 comparisons – a tedious task, even if the scoring were to be computerised. Job classification schemes, in which jobs are slotted into categories on the basis of generalised job descriptions, are not satisfactory unless the jobs can be matched readily against what are usually no more than a dozen categorised descriptions. The evaluation of a large number of disparate jobs requires some form of analytical, factor-based scheme

- How complex is the pay structure? Simple structures do not require complex scoring systems. If there are only three pay grades, the scoring system can be relatively coarse. But with 12 to 15 pay grades covering a variety of jobs, the scoring system will need to be much more refined in order to identify relatively small differences between fairly similar jobs. There should also be an interaction between job scores and the pay structure. If the scores tend to form a number of clusters, these provide a strong indication of where to place the boundaries of pay bands.

- What are the factors or characteristics to which the organisation wishes to allocate monetary value within the pay structure? Job evaluation can be a powerful tool to demonstrate the importance that an organisation places on specific competencies. The use of different factors or factor weightings can produce dramatically altered scores for the same jobs. For example, when the national job evaluation scheme for a million local government workers was designed in 1987, the traditional emphasis on physical effort and working conditions was downgraded and more weight given to the skills involved in caring for people. Consequently, the relative pay of refuse collectors and home-help workers was reversed – with the previously lower-paid home helpers scoring 630 points against the refuse collectors' 272 points.

There is also little point in including factors for which all the jobs can be assumed to have roughly equal weight. For instance, when introducing a scheme for professional employees, one organisation decided to omit the commonly used know-how factor on the grounds that it only employed people with approximately equal professional knowledge. It decided that only two factors were of critical importance: the scale of each job's output, relative to the overall size of the organisation; and the impact of good or poor individual performance on the organisation's public reputation.

If a strong emphasis is placed on using factors that are highly specific to the organisation, it is questionable whether any proprietary scheme will be wholly appropriate. The factors and factor weightings used by these schemes are inevitably standardised, so they do not necessarily reflect the values of any one organisation. Nevertheless, the fact that there are a number of job evaluation schemes on the market does provide a degree of choice, as the factors and weightings used by different systems vary widely. Any employer considering the use of a proprietary system should examine the extent to which it reflects the organisation's priorities in terms of the qualities it wishes its reward system to reflect or encourage:

- Is the scheme intended for making market comparisons? One of the arguments for using some proprietary systems is that the providers maintain a database of salaries of jobs with similar scores. The theory is that, say, engineering jobs scoring 600 points are broadly comparable across all the companies in the database. Salary analyses showing the range and median salaries for jobs with this score may therefore provide useful comparable data. Factors to consider in using such data are: whether the number of comparators in the database is sufficient to give a true picture of the market; whether the evaluation standards are common among all users; and the extent to which average figures conceal a wide range of salary levels.
- Is there an advantage in using a computerised system? An increasing number of proprietary analytical schemes are available in a computerised form. Most operate on the basis of a standardised and detailed job questionnaire, the answers to which are processed by computer to produce the necessary points scores and pay grades. The main advantages are consistency of job analysis and some saving in administration. It is important to recognise, however, that the use of a computer does not make job evaluation more objective. The questions and scores imply qualitative assumptions about the values of different factors, and producing the answers still requires some judgement.

What are the implementation costs? There are two forms of implementation expense: those concerned with the initial design or purchase of the scheme, and those arising from the results of the process. Michael Armstrong and Angela Baron of the IPD quote consultancy costs at 1995 prices of around £15,000 for a system covering 200 employees, rising to £120,000 for a large scheme, with licence fees of up to £10,000 for any software package. They also suggest that payroll increases are seldom less than 3 per cent when a scheme is first launched, because upgraded employees have to be paid more, while employees in downgraded jobs are usually red-circled.

Further information

1. ACAS, *Job Evaluation: An introduction*. London, Advisory, Conciliation and Arbitration Service, 1994.
2. ARMSTRONG M. *and* BARON A. *The Job Evaluation Handbook*. London, Institute of Personnel and Development, 1995.

15   Salary structures

There have been a number of influences in recent years which have led to an increase in the number of organisations designing their own pay systems. These include the erosion of national collective bargaining in parts of the private and public sectors, the simplification of pay and grading structures that are too complex for the slimmer and more flexible organisations of the 1990s, the harmonisation of blue-collar and white-collar pay systems and the impact of equal pay legislation.

In addition to responding to these general influences, there are three main reasons for ensuring that an organisation's salary structure is well designed:

- The salary system is more than an administration framework for controlling employee costs. The nature of the salary structure conveys messages to employees about the organisation's culture, its view of the value of jobs and of what is important in terms of performance and quality.
- Employee attitudes are affected significantly by

their views about the equity of internal pay differentials. What their colleagues are paid relative to their own pay is as important to many employees as any comparison with pay in other organisations.

- The organisation's external reputation as an employer – and therefore its ability to recruit – is also influenced by the quality of the salary structure. The absence of any apparent logic or system in the way jobs are valued can damage external perceptions of an otherwise good employer, as well as pay levels which do not reflect market realities.

There are five main stages in the design of salary structure:

1 Rank the jobs by their overall size or importance.
2 Decide how jobs should be grouped for salary purposes.
3 Define the differentials between groups or scales.
4 Define the width of each pay scale (this chapter assumes that scales, rather than single-point salaries, are to be used).
5 Assign monetary values to each scale.

Job ranking

Whether or not a formal system of job evaluation is used, decisions have to be made about the relative size or importance of all the jobs to be included in the pay structure. In the absence of any current structure or re-evaluation, existing individual salaries might be used to produce this ranking, although this cannot be recommended as good practice.

Ideally the design of a structure starts with job evaluation, and one result of equal pay legislation is to promote the use of a bias-free, factor-based evaluation systems. The primary purpose of job evaluation is to produce a rational ranking of jobs – ie the internal differentiation of jobs by their relative size. Of itself, job evaluation does not determine either the shape of the salary structure or monetary pay levels, but it does provide a systematic and rational basis for making these decisions.

Job grouping

Having ranked the jobs, the next step is to decide how they should be grouped into salary scales. In rare cases each job may be so different in size as to merit its own individual scale, but normally there are a number of jobs which differ to only a minor degree and are therefore best grouped together. Jobs which differ in evaluated point scores by less than 10 to 15 per cent rarely justify being placed in different pay scales.

There can be several options for the number of groups or scales to be used, depending on the number of clusters of jobs with the same or similar job scores, the extent to which staff are interchangeable between jobs (the greater the interchangeability, the fewer the scales), the degree of difference in job sizes (the greater the range of job size, the more the scales) and the organisation's culture (the more egalitarian, or the flatter the hierarchy, the fewer the scales). The scale boundaries are also best drawn at places in the ranking chart that form natural breaks between clusters of jobs. The aim should be to avoid very minor differences in job scores resulting in jobs being placed in different grades.

Scale differentials

A view then needs to be taken of the size of the salary differential between the scales, usually calculated at the scale mid-points. This is influenced partially by the number of scales: the fewer the scales the larger the differentials. There are two other important considerations. First, large differentials – say 30 per cent or more – will generate perceptions of major distinctions in the value to the organisation of different jobs. Small differentials, say of about 10 per cent, will reduce such status distinctions but may lead to dissatisfaction if job differences are perceived to be greater than the salary system indicates. Secondly, differentials do not have to be standard throughout the whole structure. They may be set at about 15 per cent at the lower end, increasing to 30 per cent to 40 per cent for senior management scales.

Scale width

The width of each pay scale then has to be decided, usually expressed in terms of the percentage by which scale maxima exceed scale minima. This part of the structure's design involves consideration of several factors.

In conventional public sector incremental scales (which are increasingly being phased out) scale width is usually quite restricted – in the 8–12 per cent range. The rationale for such narrow scales is that salary increases based solely on service should be relatively small. If, alternatively, salary progression is to be based on performance or competence assessments and the organisation wishes to use the salary system to emphasise the importance of individual performance standards, scale maxima may well be as much as 50 per cent above minima. In broadbanded systems, scale width may be even greater.

Wide scales inevitably involve overlap between each scale and the next, particularly if the differentials between scales are in the 10–20 per cent range. The argument for overlapping scales is that an experienced and highly competent employee in one grade is of more immediate value to the organisation than an inexperienced employee in the next higher grade. A view needs to be taken as to how sustainable this argument is if staff discontent is to be avoided, particularly if it might involve new managers being paid less than some of their experienced subordinate staff.

If a large number of different jobs are grouped for salary purposes, the number of scales will be relatively small, and it will be desirable to provide for a fairly wide range of pay within each scale. Scale widths of at least 30 per cent are common in such circumstances. One approach which has been adopted quite extensively is to use wide scales and consider each scale to be in three segments. Inexperienced staff are recruited into the bottom third of each scale; progression to the top of the middle third is normal for competent staff; movement into and through the upper third is restricted to high performers.

Setting values on scales

The final stage is to set monetary values for the minima and maxima of the various salary scales. A preliminary point is that there does not have to be a directly proportional relationship between the points scores of a job evaluation exercise and actual salaries. For example, the lowest scale may cover jobs with an average score of, say,

300 points; the highest scale may include jobs averaging 1,200 points. The fact that this highest score is four times that of the lowest does not mean that salaries for the highest scale should be four times those of the lowest. The right salary for this scale may be more or less, and the statistical relationship between evaluation scores and salaries needs to be calculated after the lower and upper salary limits have been set.

The primary determinant of salary values should be the organisation's view of where it wishes to be in the market, which involves first obtaining market data and then making a policy decision as to where the organisation's salaries should be pitched, taking into account such factors as recruitment and retention experience and the range of costs of non-pay benefits. It is no easy task to mount a comprehensive salary survey covering several different types and levels of jobs. Jobs need to be very carefully defined if accurate comparative information is to be obtained, and there is always the possibility that competitors will not be willing to share their salary data. An alternative is to participate in a salary club. There are a number of groups of employers – sometimes national, more often regional – who agree to exchange salary information. Inquiries among colleagues in the local IPD branch will often produce information about the existence of these clubs.

Some of the large consultancies maintain extensive comparative salary data collected from clients who subscribe to a regular information and updating service. Some are linked to the use of the particular consultancy's job evaluation system. Useful salary data can also be obtained from general pay surveys and reports.

What any survey will reveal is that there is no clear-cut market rate. A decision will therefore be needed as to where the organisation's salary levels should be pitched. It is normal to use the mid-point of the salary scales as the point of comparison and to set this against a defined point in the market range. This is usually described in terms of medians (mid-point), deciles (upper or lower 10 per cent) or quartiles (upper or lower 25 per cent). Many organisations aim to stay at the median, but there may be good reasons for selecting a higher or lower position.

Once this decision has been made, the mid-point salary values of the scales can be set and the scale minima and maxima calculated to produce the desired scale-width. In practice, precise market-related salaries rarely result in a smooth progression of scale values, and some adjustments will be necessary to produce a statistically consistent set of scales. It may also be necessary to introduce market supplements for those jobs which the evaluation process places in scales well below the market rates.

Further reading

ARMSTRONG M. *Employee Reward*. London, Institute of Personnel and Development, 1996.

16   Rewarding performance

Linking pay to performance is a firmly established feature of reward management in the private sector and has been introduced quite widely, although not universally, in local authorities and Civil Service agencies. Most managers feel instinctively that money is a motivator, even though research evidence to support this is far from conclusive.

There are, though, other reasons for rewarding performance than simple motivation. For example, the absence of performance payments may be seen as unfair to high performers who earn no more than low performers in the same jobs. Equity rather than motivation may then be the objective of a reward scheme.

Performance pay may also help to ensure that managers take the performance assessments of their staff seriously. Without this positive outcome, the annual appraisal may become little more than a routine administrative chore. But if managers are accountable for the effective distribution of significant performance-pay budgets, they are more likely to ensure their staff's appraisals are thorough and well founded. Performance pay has also (though unwisely) been used to boost basic pay to market levels.

Financial payments are not the only form of performance reward. Non-cash methods are available, ranging from informal, verbal commendations to elaborate schemes for gift vouchers or overseas travel. The recognition of good performance is perhaps more important than the precise form of the reward. If employees see that good work is expected, recognised and commended, a performance-conscious culture develops. There is certainly no one best type or method of rewarding performance.

Nevertheless, it is important for any formal reward system to be cost-effective and consistent with the organisation's management systems and culture. There is also one general precondition: no reward system will be considered credible by employees unless decisions about rewards are seen to be based on fair and objective assessments of performance against predetermined criteria. The effect of performance payments (or other rewards) which appear to employees to be the result of capricious judgements by individual managers can be far worse than the absence of any type of performance-linked reward. Effective rewards systems therefore need to be subsidiary to clearly articulated systems of performance management and appraisal which are understood and respected by the employees covered.

Financial rewards

The many forms of financial rewards can be grouped into four categories:

- salary increases within normal pay scales – probably the most commonly used form. It conveys a simple message to employees that the job is worth between £x and £y, depending on how well it is done, and that any pay progression between the minimum and maximum is dependent on achieving at least a satisfactory level of performance. Exceptional performers may move through the scale more rapidly, but everyone's pay progression is clearly performance-related.

salary increases above the maxima of normal scales. This form of payment has been adopted by some public sector bodies that are retaining conventional incremental pay scales but adding performance payments to them. The message to employees is somewhat different from the first category. Here, the system is saying that basically satisfactory performance will lead automatically to the normal scale maxima, but exceptional performance will be paid above the normal level. So only high performers benefit, and this may be seen as a disadvantage from a motivational viewpoint

increases to single-point salaries, a form of payment commonly used by organisations which do not use pay scales and do not negotiate a general annual pay rise. Each employee is paid at a fixed rate, but this is subject to annual review. The organisation budgets for a general percentage increase in the paybill, but the amount by which each employee's pay is increased is decided by performance assessment. Poor performers may receive nothing. This is a powerful form of reward, unless inflation or market forces generate a need for a general uplift in pay of a size which swamps the performance message

■ lump-sum payments not incorporated into salary. This type of reward can be used as an addition to almost any salary system. It has consequently been introduced by some public-sector bodies that are retaining incremental scales, as well as by private sector organisations with fixed-point salaries that are uprated only for inflation. Different levels of performance generate lump-sum bonuses of varying sizes. One argument for this form of reward is that a lump sum has much more impact than the same amount of money merged into salary and spread over 12 monthly salary payments. It also avoids the problems which can occur with salary-based payments when performance deteriorates. This was the type of performance pay preferred by the majority of respondents in the IPM's extensive 1990 survey of older employees' attitudes.

There are also hybrid schemes which use more than one of the preceding methods. Several schemes use performance progression within pay scales until high-performing staff reach their grade maxima and then pay lump sums. Lump sums are sometimes used to reward specific pieces of meritorious work, while performance increments are used to reward sustained overall performance. Other schemes may use automatic incremental progression to the mid-point of the pay scales, and performance progression thereafter.

The size of performance payments relative to basic salary also has to be considered. This should be influenced by the organisation's history and culture and by how the awards are communicated. It can be argued that, if performance pay is just being introduced in an organisation with a long history of automatic increments, relatively small sums will make a considerable impact because of their novelty. But a company which has always operated a performance pay system and now wants to refresh its scheme will almost certainly need to increase the size of its performance payments – or introduce new forms of non-financial rewards to regenerate interest.

More impact can be given to small sums by the way they are announced. A standard note from the pay section informing the employees that their monthly salary has been increased by £33.33 as a result of the annual performance assessment may not do much to raise enthusiasm. A personally presented letter from the managing director saying, 'Well done, and as a token of recognition of your good performance I am pleased to enclose a cheque for £400' is likely to have a much greater effect.

Non-financial rewards

Non-financial rewards are incentives (or demonstrations of recognition) in kind rather than cash. They fall broadly into two categories: commendations and gifts or vouchers.

As regards commendations, the motivational impact of a manager saying 'well done' to an employee when a good piece of work has been completed should not be underestimated, regardless of the existence of more formal reward procedures. Using the annual appraisal to commend good performance, rather than it being seen as a fault-finding exercise, is also important. Commendations can be given more impact by written confirmation of oral praise, or letters of commendation from a senior manager. Even a simple note along the following lines will be much more appreciated than many managers realise:

> I am very pleased to confirm what I said this morning about the excellent work you have put into the ABC project, and I am putting this note on your personal file. Your energy and enthusiasm for results have helped to make this project a great success – well done and thank you for a sterling effort.

The two main forms of gifts for performance are overseas travel and consumer items such as cameras or jewellery. Traditionally, this type of reward has been used almost exclusively for sales staff – often as a prize for achieving the best sales record. But in recent years there has been an extension of such rewards beyond the sales force to a wide variety of other occupational groups, including manual employees. This type of reward is also being used to recognise team performance, for example, with whole sections of employees going on an overseas trip as a reward for co-operating with a major organisational or locational change.

There are a number of practical questions to consider before starting to use rewards of this kind:

- Should the management decide on the gifts (or travel destinations), or should employees be given vouchers so they can choose for themselves? Most employees prefer vouchers, though this may limit the ability for the organisation to arrange a group travel event or a high-profile presentation ceremony.

- What are the tax implications and how are these to be handled? Generally, awards of these kinds are taxable for their full value as income, although there are a number of complications, depending on whether gifts or vouchers are used and on the salary of the employee. Similar complications exist with National Insurance liability, and organisations should seek specialist advice before embarking on any gift or voucher scheme. There are three ways of meeting tax liability: it may be left to the employee, covered by the employer by grossing up the amount for PAYE, or handled through a taxed award scheme under the auspices of the Inland Revenue incentive valuation unit.

- What are the costs? In addition to the direct costs of gifts or vouchers (including tax liabilities if the employer decides to meet these), it is advisable to budget for the costs of publicising and administering the scheme. Somewhere between 10 per cent and 20 per cent above basic costs may be required if extensive publicity is to be used and if lavish presentation events are organised.

There is a two-fold case for using non-financial rewards. It can be argued that the presentation of a gift or voucher makes much more impact than any form of cash payment, particularly a pay increase which is merged with monthly salary payment. And a highly publicised scheme, with attractive awards or prizes, generates much more excitement and sense of fun than the rather bureaucratic characteristics of most financial reward schemes.

Non-financial rewards may also be more suitable than

monetary payments when the objective is to reward a team, rather than an individual – particularly when the reward is for a team's success on a time-limited project. Companies use events such as a team visit to a theme park or a group flight on Concorde for this type of reward, while team recognition through the award of prizes and titles ('Champion sales team of the year') are also common, particularly when an element of competition can be encouraged between teams. The principle of team recognition can be extended to almost any work in which performance is essentially dependent on collective effort within clearly defined teams, and may include some form of team bonuses, separate from salaries and based on measurable financial outcomes, where this is practicable.

Further reading

1 ARMSTRONG M. *Employee Reward*. London, Institute of Personnel and Development, 1996.

2 ARMSTRONG M. *and* BARON A. *Performance Management: The new realities.* London, Institute of Personnel and Development, 1998.

3 *The IPD Guide on Team Reward.* London, Institute of Personnel and Development, 1996.

17   Flexible benefits

The concept of giving employees an individual choice of benefits, rather than providing a standardised package, has been discussed in personnel circles for many years but is only slowly being put into practice. The case for flexibility is based on a recognition that employees' personal circumstances, and the value to them of different elements in the employment package, vary greatly between individuals. For the same total cost as a standard package, a flexible or cafeteria system might generate greater employee satisfaction and thus contribute more effectively to recruitment, retention and motivation. The increasing number of organisations that are now giving the idea serious consideration need to address several issues:

- flexibility within single benefits
- costing the benefits which might be flexed
- selecting the employee group for participation
- selecting the benefits for flexing
- the tax implications for employees and the employer
- scheme administration.

Flexibility in single benefits

Before embarking on a full-scale flexible (or cafeteria) benefits system, it is worth considering what scope exists for providing flexibility within the provision of individual benefits. The three most common examples are working hours, car benefits and pension provisions.

Flexible working hours provide employees with some choice in daily working time. Annual hours contracts can introduce work-time flexibility over time spans of a week or more, or on a seasonal basis. A more radical approach may include an option for at least partial home-based working.

Choice can be built into company car schemes. The simplest measure is to provide cars through a car-leasing supplier, and allow a wide choice of car for a set annual leasing cost. Other options may include choosing a less expensive car and taking the balance in cash; or paying extra to have a larger car. The wider option of choosing cash instead of a company car is referred to later in this chapter.

Pension scheme options, in addition to the normal AVC (additional voluntary contributions) provisions may include a choice in the level of individual employee contributions (say, between 3 per cent and 6 per cent), linked to a similar range of employer contributions, and some trade-off between normal pension benefits and linked benefits such as widows' pensions or death benefit.

Costing the benefits

The financial principle behind a flexible benefits system is that, whatever choices each employee makes, the total cost of each package will be the same for the same category or level of employee. So there needs to be an accurate costing of each benefit in order to assess the extent to which reducing one can be offset by increasing another. It is particularly important to decide what value to attribute to a day's work, so that any potential trade-off between annual leave and other benefits is properly costed.

Typical costs for an employee currently on a salary of about £25,000, are shown in the table, below:

Salary and NI contributions	
during 219 working days:	£21,420
during 8 days' public holiday:	£783
during 25 days' annual leave:	£2,445
during 8 days' sick leave:	£783
Company pension contributions:	£1,428
Company car leasing cost:	£3,570
Business mileage fuel costs:	£571
Private family medical insurance:	£392
Annual health screening:	£297
Accident and life insurance:	£120
Telephone allowance:	£140
Payment of professional subscriptions:	£120
Interest on season ticket loan:	£120
Cost of subsidised catering:	£595
TOTAL	£32,784

This table shows that benefits may well amount to 30 per cent or more of base salary. A number of possible options can be considered from this kind of schedule. For example, if the employee chose to opt out of private medical insurance, the finance released for other benefits might be used to increase the employer's pension contribution by 1.6 per cent of basic salary.

In assessing costs, particular care needs to be paid to the possible effect on unit costs of significant numbers of employees opting out of benefits such as medical insurance. Smaller numbers might well result in higher premiums. The possibility that the take-up of some benefits, such as life insurance, might be skewed towards a particular age group should also be considered. The cost of benefits of this kind vary with age, and it cannot be assumed that current costs, averaged over the whole workforce, would apply after introducing choice. It is advisable to run an employee survey to discover likely outcomes of various options before finalising a scheme.

Selecting the employee group

Different benefits may have different relative values at different status or salary levels, and it may not be considered appropriate to offer some benefits to all staff. For these reasons, a number of schemes have been limited to managerial grades, although the trend towards single-status employment should make it easier to introduce flexible benefits on a company-wide basis.

While limiting the application of a scheme to senior grades can ease some of the costing and administrative problems, it may generate resentment among other employees. Given that one objective in introducing flexible benefits is to improve staff motivation, the effect on morale of launching a restricted scheme certainly needs to be a factor in any assessment of the pros and cons of a potential scheme. And if differentiation between categories is considered necessary, it might be possible to introduce at least some form of flexibility for groups that might otherwise be excluded.

Selecting the benefits

The next major decision is what to include in the flexible package. Total flexibility is not practicable. For example, without some limitation it would be possible, in the example given in the table, for an employee to exchange car, pension and healthcare benefits for an additional 60 days' annual leave – an obviously absurd outcome.

This shows that, although the costs of benefits provide a standard form of comparison, factors other than finance need to be considered. In some schemes, choice is limited to groups of benefits which have some broad relationship – such as insurance schemes for dental and medical treatment, long-term illness, death benefits and ill-health retirement pensions. Within the same scheme, there may be separate cash-for-car options and the limited sale or purchase of days of leave.

Cash may be used, within defined limits, as a general-purpose option, and a cash-for-car choice is becoming increasingly common (although not necessarily within a wider scheme of flexible benefits). An important point to assess when costing this option is the additional travel costs which may occur when employees have to be paid full mileage rates for using their own cars, instead of just petrol costs when using a company car.

A more controversial and less common option is the purchase or sale of days of leave, with employees either opting to reduce their leave entitlement for more salary, or taking more leave for a salary reduction. This highlights the need to place limits on the extent of flexibility for any one benefit. Organisations that allow trading in annual leave set maxima on the number of days that can be either bought or sold, perhaps five days a year on either side of the standard leave allowance. Also, additional days' leave may be priced at a premium (say, 20 per cent) above the standard daily wage costs. Limits may also have to be set on benefits such as company pension contributions or share options to meet legal or tax requirements.

Tax implications

Assessing the impact of tax is a crucially important aspect, as the relative value of various benefits to the individual employee is strongly influenced by the Inland Revenue's assessment of their tax status. This is not a matter to be left to amateurs, and specialist advice is essential. Schedule E tax regulations apply, but regard should also be paid to regional tax inspectors' interpretations and to precedents set by the courts.

The tax situation is continually changing, although there is a trend towards reducing the tax advantages of benefits in kind. The principle is the conversion of non-pay benefits into a notional cash equivalent, which is then taxed on a PAYE basis. This trend has major implications for the future of company cars but may also lead to a more general focus on cash-for-benefit options. Expert advice may also be needed to ensure compliance with other regulations about pension contributions and benefits, share options, and payments under profit-related pay schemes.

Scheme administration

Flexible benefits are more complex to administer than a standard package. This is not necessarily an argument for restricting choice, but it is vital that effective processes and controls are put in place before embarking on a scheme. A particular point to consider is the purpose of a scheme. This is generally to generate commitment and motivation and it will not be achieved unless the aims, value and details of the scheme are clearly explained and promoted. Extensive employee communication is essential and, in a scheme of any complexity, it is helpful to provide a facility for employees to obtain financial counselling.

Clear rules are needed on the two key aspects of the scheme: the credit that each employee may spend on the benefits in the package, and the option price of each benefit, together with any limits on choice. A procedure is needed to handle changes in employees' options, coupled with a decision about how often employees may vary their choice. A potential problem is that employees' personal circumstances change, and what was an attractive option at one time may become unsatisfactory at a later date. Frequent changes of choice also create major administrative and cost control difficulties. Some organisations allow their employees to change their selection of benefits only at one set date each year, or define different durations for individual benefits during which no change is permitted.

Further information

ARMSTRONG M. *Reward Management*. London, Kogan Page, 1996.

18   Childcare assistance

Employers' provision of various forms of assistance with childcare is slowly increasing as a response to the growing number of women with young children who are either seeking employment or who wish to remain in work after a short maternity break. Organisations are realising that childcare measures can reduce the loss of experienced staff, which occurs when women leave to have children and do not return. A Midland Bank survey showed the percentage of women returners increasing from 30 per cent to 80 per cent when childcare assistance was provided. However, children assistance is still provided by only a minority of employers. Only about 12% of private-sector employers made some form of childcare provision, while childcare vouchers (arguably the most cost-effective form of financial assistance) are issued by only about 200 organisations across the public and private sectors.

Provision of childcare can take several forms:

- workplace nurseries
- buying places at other nurseries

- childcare allowances and childcare vouchers
- information and advisory services
- holiday play schemes and after-school clubs.

The trend for primary schools to take in children under 5 years of age is also significant, and the government now guarantees a nursery place being available (at a school or nursery) for every 4-year-old.

This guarantee was part of the government's £300 million childcare package, announced in the 1998 budget, which aims to provide 20,000 more out-of-school places and to increase the number of after-school clubs from about 3000 to 30,000 – providing one million places at these clubs. Childcare tax credits will also come into effect from the 2000/2001 tax year – easing the burden of childcare costs for lower-earning families.

Nurseries

For many working parents, the most satisfactory form of childcare assistance would be the day nursery on the employer's premises. Parent and child can travel to and from the workplace together, there can be contact with the child at meal breaks, and it is also a tax-free benefit. Unfortunately, the cost rules out this option for most employers. Nurseries are expensive to set up and run, and unless the employer is prepared to subsidise the costs at a high level, the charges made to employees may be higher then most non-managerial staff can afford. Weekly charges by a number of large companies range from about £50 to £160. Start-up costs can be around £1,200 per child, and annual running costs for a 25-place nursery some £6000 per child. Nurseries must also be registered with the relevant local authority's social services department and are subject to annual inspection.

One way of reducing costs is for several employers in the same location to form a partnership and share the facilities of a single nursery. Many employers with nurseries also provide the premises and equipment, but contract out the running of the nursery to a specialist operator. A simpler way of providing nursery facilities is for the employer to buy places at a local nursery. While this method relieves the employer of start-up costs and any form of nursery management, it is not a low-cost alternative to a workplace nursery. The charges, even at a reduced block-booking rate, will still be at commercial levels. If the employer then subsidises these rates to employees, the value of the subsidy is subject to tax – unlike subsidies for workplace nurseries – although £70 per week childcare tax credits will change the current tax position radically from April 2000.

When some form of nursery facility is provided it becomes necessary to define employees' eligibility. Some organisations operate on a first-come, first-served basis, so the employees who secure places will not necessarily be those with the greatest need. Other employers give priority to employees in certain job categories, particularly those involving key skills for which recruitment is difficult. This may be linked to an assessment of personal circumstances, such as priority for those returning from maternity leave. Equal opportunity legislation makes it unlawful to restrict eligibility to women or to people of any marital status. Some organisations have set up allocation committees with management and employee membership to make decisions about eligibility in individual cases.

Allowances and vouchers

The simplest form of assistance, particularly for organisations that are too small to consider nursery provision, is the payment of childcare allowances to eligible employees who are incurring private childcare costs. Eligibility criteria used by employers making these payments include:

- salary limits, with payments made only to employees earning less than a defined maximum, which in some cases is as low as £15,000
- children's age limits – most schemes are limited to childcare for children under school age, although a minority of schemes extend this to age 14 or 16
- length of service, with some organisations requiring employees to have completed at least one or two years' service
- priorities for certain categories such as women returnees or single parents
- a restriction to employees using registered childminders or nurseries.

It is also normal to pay allowances pro rata for eligible part-timers; to restrict payments to one child per employee at any one time; and to pay only against proof of expenditure. Allowances average about £32 per week, in a range of between £20 and £50. Childcare allowances are still treated as taxable income and also count for National Insurance contributions.

Some organisations operate a cash-limited childcare allowance fund from which payments are made to approved applicants. There may be a joint panel of management and employee representatives who decide, within agreed principles, which applicants should receive payments, and for what sums. Single parents on low incomes are likely to be given a high priority. Childcare vouchers can be purchased by the employer from what is currently the only issuing company – Childcare Vouchers Ltd. They are then issued to eligible employees, who can use them to purchase almost any form of childcare. The employee gives the voucher to the childcare provider who then cashes it through the issuing company. The employer decides what value of vouchers to provide, and sets the eligibility criteria.

Vouchers offer several advantages over cash allowances. Vouchers can only be exchanged for childcare, so the employer knows that the money is being spent on its intended purpose. Vouchers are kept separate from salaries, and are consequently a very visible sign of the employer's commitment to childcare assistance. They do not count for employer or employee National Insurance contributions, and are deductible expenses for corporation tax purposes, though they are a taxable benefit under PAYE. The exemption from employers' National Insurance contributions is partially offset by service charges to the issuing company. These vary, depending on the number of employees involved, the price level of the vouchers and the number of weeks in the year in which vouchers were issued. In practice, the average weekly value of vouchers currently being issued is very similar to the average for cash allowances. The eligibility criteria which organisations use for voucher schemes is also generally the same, or very similar, to those used for cash allowances.

Information and advice

Many parents may not be aware of the various sources of information and advice on childcare, or be unsure which would be best to help them with any particular problem or query. One organisation – Childcare Solutions – provides a consolidated service by which parents, through a single freephone contact, can obtain information on almost every aspect of childcare. This includes advice on general parenting matters, as well as information about childminders, nurseries, holiday schemes and the new government childcare programme. The scheme is available only to parents working for employers who participate in the scheme. The service is provided free to all Childcare Voucher clients, but can be purchased separately by other employers for an annual fee. The scheme is a relatively low-cost method of giving some help to working parents without incurring the much higher costs of allowances, vouchers or nursery subsidies, and without having to impose any restrictive eligibility criteria.

Play schemes and after-school clubs

Nurseries, cash allowances and vouchers are generally limited to children under school age, but the provision of care for older children may still be a problem. School days are shorter than full-time working days, and the school holidays are longer than employees' annual leave. Organised care for children after school is not something employers are normally able to assist with, although it may be helpful to give employees information about any local initiatives provided by schools and the Kids Clubs Network.

A recent development has been the Out of School Childcare Grant scheme of the Department for Education and Employment. The grant is paid to local TECs to help develop a range of out-of-school facilities in their areas, and some schools and local education authorities are now providing various free play and activity programmes during school holidays. An expansion of this scheme is part of the new government childcare programme.

Some employers also run holiday play schemes, either directly or with the assistance of Kids Clubs, sometimes on a partnership basis with other local employers. Company sports and social facilities may provide a good venue for these schemes, although any scheme for eight or more children has to be registered with the relevant social services department. When charges are made, these average £8 to £15 per day.

Further information

1 IDS. *Childcare.* Study No. 633. London, Incomes Data Services, 1997.

2 CHILDCARE VOUCHERS AND CHILDCARE SOLUTIONS: 50 Vauxhall Bridge Road, London SW1V 2RS (0171 834 6666).

3 NATIONAL CHILDMINDING ASSOCIATION: 8 Masons Hill, Bromley, Kent BR2 9EY (0181 464 6164).

4 PARENTS AT WORK: 45 Beech Street, London EC2Y 8AD (0171 628 3565).

5 KIDS CLUBS NETWORK, 3 Muirfield Crescent, London, E14 9SZ (0171 512 1212).

19   Company cars

During the 1970s and 1980s a competitive recruitment situation, coupled with the favourable tax treatment of car benefits, led to the large-scale expansion of provision of company cars. The later recession resulted in some reduction in this provision, while more recently a steady increase in the proportion of car benefit assessed for tax has reduced the attractiveness of the company car. Two specific reactions to these trends have been:

- an increasing use of a benefit option in which the employee can opt for extra cash as an alternative to a car
- the provision of smaller cars and the use of longer car leasing periods. It is probably wise to plan on the assumption that in the long term, all tax advantages will be phased out.

Yet despite the diminishing tax advantages, the provision of a company car is likely to be seen by many employees as an attractive benefit for other than specific tax reasons for a long time to come. In private ownership, few people make adequate provision for replacement costs, so tax deductions for a company car may feel less painful than writing large cheques for hire purchase payments from post-tax income. There is also a significant convenience factor in not having to deal with repairs and maintenance, particularly in schemes that provide a replacement vehicle at these times.

It is therefore likely that many organisations will continue to provide cars for recruitment, retention and motivational reasons, even if tax advantages disappear. This indicates a need to ensure that car policies are cost-effective, and in any review of these policies, the following main questions arise:

- Should cars be limited to jobs in which the frequent use of a car is essential?
- If not, how widely should cars be provided simply as an attractive element in the employment package?
- To what extent should the type of car be related to job status?
- Should employees eligible for cars have a choice – either between different cars, or between a car allowance and additional salary?
- What method of car provision should be used (eg purchase, leasing etc)?
- What are the employers' tax and National Insurance implications?

Essential use

From a purely operational viewpoint there is no case for providing cars other than for jobs in which the car is a tool of the trade. But a complication arises because the car used at work is of equal use at home. Once private use is permitted for some employees (the essential car users) others will see this as favourable treatment and will seek the same benefit. To that extent, providing cars on a more general basis may be justified as the provision of equal treatment.

An alternative is to permit private use but charge the employee for it. A more common practice is to permit free private use but require the employee to cover private fuel costs. (Free private fuel is assessable for tax.) If pool cars are operated, it may be possible to eliminate private usage by making cars available from the pool only when business journeys are necessary. Against all these measures may be the view that cars need to be provided more widely as part of an attractive employment package.

Eligibility and status

Assuming the decision is to provide cars on a wider basis than strict business need, there are two points to consider:

- How is eligibility to be defined?
- What differences, if any, in car type should be provided for different categories of eligible employees?

The two broad ways of defining eligibility are by salary or grade level and by job category. The public sector tends to use the former, with all staff above a certain grade becoming eligible. Many companies use the latter. Both approaches place limits on car provision, with lower-level employees almost always excluded. Wherever the line is drawn it needs to be recognised that recruitment and retention advantages for eligible staff may be offset to some extent by disgruntlement among those employees just the wrong side of the line.

Many companies link the type (or value) of car to levels in the management hierarchy. So directors have Daimlers, senior managers BMWs, middle managers Omegas – and so on. There are two problems with this very common approach:

- The hierarchy may be more complex than the range of cars that can sensibly be provided, and cars then form a separate status grouping which does not equate to the company structure. Differences in car provision which are not perceived as justified by real status distinctions can then be a potent source of discontent.
- If it is decided that to project a good company image a car costing, say, £14,000 needs to be provided to the least senior level of staff, this sets a high cost base for the whole car hierarchy. Some organisations are responding to these problems by using variants of the same model to reduce (though not eliminate) the differences between cars and to lower the average car cost.

Providing choice

There are three reasons for providing choice of some kind. The first is that cost savings may be achieved if some employees opt out of high-value, low mileage cars which may no longer be tax-efficient. Secondly, status symbolism may be reduced by employees choosing salary instead of cars, or choosing smaller cars. The third reason is that the provision of choice may well itself be an attractive feature for some employees – there is a growing interest in the concept of flexible benefits, of which this may be a part. Four types of choice can be considered:

- a choice of car within a designated range or price band. This is frequently used in car leasing schemes in which employees are told the annual leasing charge the company will meet, and they may then choose any car the leasing company can provide at this figure
- an option for the employee to top up the designated leasing sum to obtain a more expensive vehicle – or choose a lower-cost car and take the balance of the leasing charge in cash. This system helps to minimise the status distinctions
- the choice of cash instead of a car – either as an addition to salary or as a separate car allowance
- car allowances which include an element for using a private car on company business obtain more favourable tax treatment than straight additions to salary.

Methods of car provision

The main methods of car provision are full purchase, hire purchase, contract hire (leasing) and contract purchase. Running a company-owned car fleet is a costly operation, involving capital investment and the skills and costs of fleet management. But a major reason for opting for a company-owned car fleet is that large discounts are available to fleet buyers. A variant is for the company to purchase and retain ownership of its cars, but to contract out their management to a specialist fleet management company.

With hire purchase, the finance company retains ownership of the vehicles. This avoids tying up capital and there are some company tax advantages in relation to interest charges. Disadvantages include having to arrange for maintenance, repairs, insurance and road tax, and the risk of incurring a loss when the vehicle is eventually disposed of.

With contract hire or leasing, the rental normally includes maintenance, repairs, insurance and road tax, plus a recovery and replacement service. Leasing periods vary from two to five years. Ownership remains with the lessor. Advantages include minimal administration, no capital expenditure, and no problems in disposing of used vehicles. Among the disadvantages may be a higher unit cost than might be achieved with an efficiently managed system of owned cars. The method is very widely used in the public sector.

Contract purchase is a hybrid of hire purchase and car leasing. The user acquires ownership of the vehicle at the end of an agreed leasing period by a 'balloon payment', which is set at about the trade price for a used vehicle of that age. The user can then sell the car on, and if the car is in good condition will then effectively have paid only for normal depreciation and maintenance costs. The leasing company takes responsibility for maintenance during the leasing period in order to protect the eventual trade-in value. Organisations considering the use of this type of car provision should investigate the company tax position in relation to capital allowances and interest charges.

This chapter is not intended to provide a detailed guide to all the financial and tax complexities of various forms of car provision, but rather to identify the main issues involved in designing a car scheme. Professional tax and accountancy advice is essential before launching any scheme, with the variables including:

- the organisation's capital financing policy
- whether interest rates are fixed or variable
- financial penalties for returning a car to a leasing company before the end of the leasing period
- insurance costs, and their relation to the company's claims record
- eligibility for capital allowances
- tax and National Insurance implications for employer and employee
- the patterns and volumes of business mileage
- car values and engine sizes and their link with tax regulations and insurance costs.

Further information

1 MONKS PARTNERSHIP. *Annual Report on Car Policy*. Monks Partnership Ltd, updated annually.
2 NTC PUBLICATIONS, *Pay and Benefits Yearbook*. NTC Publications Ltd, updated annually.

Training them up

20 Identifying training needs

A general resurgence of attention to training in many organisations, together with national initiatives such National Vocational Qualifications (NVQs) has added emphasis to the need for the effective identification of training needs. Training can be expensive, and a faulty analysis of what training is required can result in a significant waste of company resources. More positively, an accurate training analysis enables limited training budgets to be directed towards activities that will achieve optimum benefits.

There are two broad questions for a training needs analysis to address:

- What training is needed?
- How is this best delivered?

Behind these questions there are three related issues:

- recognising the differences in training requirements between knowledge, skill and attitude
- distinguishing between individual and corporate training needs

deciding which training is best done externally and which should be done in-house, and within the in-house activity deciding on the best use of course or job-based training.

This chapter deals primarily with the first two of these issues, though it concludes with brief comments on the third point, since a training needs analysis is of little practical use if it is not converted into an effective training programme.

Knowledge, skill and attitude

Whatever methods are used in producing a training needs analysis, it is important to distinguish between the three broad reasons why training may be required; and to be clear about what constitutes a satisfactory level of knowledge, skill and attitude. The questions to ask are:

1 What do employees need to know in order to perform their jobs well? This may range from background information about the organisation to very detailed technical know-how about the individual work tasks.

2 What skills or competencies are required, and to what level? Knowledge by itself (eg of the theory of a technical process) is not enough to secure acceptable performance – tuition, coaching, planned experience or work simulations are needed to develop the necessary skills.

3 What attitudinal characteristics are needed? Of course, in all jobs the general attributes of interest, commitment and enthusiasm are important, but for a training needs analysis this aspect requires more

specific attention. There may, for example, be a need for employees to develop a particular type or set of attitudes towards customer service, technical standards, work flexibility, quality or cost-consciousness.

Individual training needs

Within any group of employees doing the same work, there will be differences in individual needs for training, influenced by differences in aptitude or previous experience. These differences need to be identified if resources are not to be wasted on a scatter-gun approach to training programmes based solely on generalisations about the whole workforce. The main methods of assessing these needs on a person-by-person basis are:

- through the performance appraisal process – with each employee's individual on-going training and development requirements being identified and then discussed at the annual appraisal interview
- in the absence of a formal appraisal process, by examining employees' individual output and quality records – a method frequently used in the manual or production sector, where inadequate training may be identified as the reason for some employees' low productivity or higher than normal reject rates
- through assessment centre techniques in which groups of employees undertake various tests and job simulation exercises under observation. Assessment centres are commonly used to identify employees with potential for promotion, but the

techniques will also indicate training needs within their current jobs

■ by questionnaires – usually with a checklist of training topics, asking employees individually whether they feel their work would benefit from further training. Supervisors or team leaders are also usually asked to complete a similar questionnaire for each member of their work group.

In both the initial analysis and in the resultant training plans, it is helpful to distinguish between immediate training needs within the employee's current job, and longer-term development needs. Employees' suggestions about their own training often focus on those courses and wider experience which might assist them in gaining a promotion or professional qualification. Supervisors' views about their staff usually concentrate on training to improve current job performance. An effective training analysis takes both types of training need into account and produces a training plan which strikes an acceptable balance.

Corporate training needs

Every organisation needs its employees to achieve, and hopefully to exceed, a basically satisfactory standard of performance, and this implies the need for a certain general level of knowledge and skill. Depending on the recruitment and selection policies for each type or group of employees, an assessment can therefore be made of the shortfall between the levels of aptitude and ability which new recruits bring to their own work and what the organisation requires. It is this shortfall that needs to be met by a corporate training policy and action programme. Selection policies are relevant as the organisation may decide to recruit only fully qualified or experienced staff, or to rely on its own trainee schemes to develop unqualified or inexperienced staff.

Future changes in skill or knowledge requirements also need to be identified when producing business plans. Human resource planning, which includes the development of recruitment and training strategies, makes sense only when it is linked directly to the whole business process. A failure to include adequate provision for training within a plan involving changes in products, services, technology or markets, is a potential cause of business failure. Other sources of data for analysis are:

- job descriptions and person specifications, in which carefully considered selection criteria for the recruitment of experienced staff provide a rich source of data about the levels of knowledge and work experience to which the training of inexperienced employees should aspire
- performance objectives and quality standards as defined in a performance management system. Quantified targets may be set for production and quality. Do employees require more training to ensure these targets are achieved? Training programmes may well form part of the action plans that are developed within the performance management system.
- analyses of competency requirements, possibly to match those NVQ or MCI standards that are

considered relevant to the various jobs involved. These can be compared with assessments of the current general levels of employee skills and abilities. This approach also has relevance in the identification of individual training needs.

▪ analysis of appraisal records, which may indicate that some training needs considered to be specific to a few individuals are in fact indicative of more general requirements. The core values of the organisation and its corporate aims are a particularly important factor when considering training to change or develop employee attitudes. For example, organisations embracing the total quality philosophy normally find it necessary to put the whole workforce through a series of quality seminars as part of the process.

Ideally, the analysis of training needs is a continuous process, drawing information from the results of performance appraisals and business plans to produce a regularly updated set of training objectives and programmes. Where this ongoing analysis has not been practised, or if business circumstances change in a major way, which necessitates a total review of current training, analysis of training needs may have to be mounted as a major project. There are four main ways of approaching this:

1 A fully comprehensive review, which would examine every aspect of every job (current or projected), and check or test every employee's level of know-how and competence for each aspect, setting these results against a projection of the

organisation's business needs. For a sizeable workforce, particularly if many different types of job are involved, this can be a formidable task.

2   To simplify the analysis, the review can concentrate on key tasks, looking only at the activities and skills that are central to the organisation's needs

3   On a more limited basis, the analysis can focus on identified difficulties or problems – what has been going wrong that better training might put right?

4   The method which might suit large, diverse organisations is for the central training function to concentrate on the identification of common or core skills – those skills that apply to all types of work across the whole organisation (eg interpersonal skills for managers, numeracy skills for many types of work, clerical skills); while the various subsidiary or operational units analyse the training needs specific to the work in their particular sectors.

It may also be helpful to produce a matrix, sub-divided into the occupations or job types, showing the different training needs for four main categories of staff: new recruits, newly promoted or transferred staff, staff in existing and unchanging jobs, and staff in jobs subject to change.

In-house or external training

Once training needs have been identified, the next step is to decide how and where these needs are best met – with an important choice between training done internally and the use of external training agencies. This chapter does not examine this issue in any detail, but among the factors to consider are:

- external training may be most appropriate for meeting knowledge and skill requirements which are not highly specific to the organisation
- external training in which the organisation's staff meet employees from other organisations can help broaden interest and understanding
- internal training may be most appropriate to meet highly specific needs; and for training designed to alter attitudes and to change or reinforce organisational culture
- the relative costs of in-house and external training are also of obvious importance – including the midway option of training being conducted in-house by external tutors
- the availability of the organisation's own managers and specialists to contribute to internal training courses, and their ability as tutors, can be a key factor. In-house training officers may be able to handle some training topics without such assistance, but for many courses the input of experienced staff is very valuable. Such staff may well require tuition in training methods and techniques.

Linked to the decision about internal or external trainers is the question of training methods. It should not be assumed that all training has to be course based. Individual training needs in particular may be best met by a variety of other means, such as: planned work experience, mentoring and coaching, personal study programmes, distance-learning packages, secondments and study visits.

Further Information

1 BOYDELL T. *and* LEARY M. *Identifying Training Needs.* London, Institute of Personnel and Development, 1996.
2 BEE F. *and* R. *Training Needs Analysis and Evaluation.* London, Institute of Personnel and Development, 1994.

21 Management training providers

The range of management training programmes offered by a variety of training providers has never been greater, with over 500 training providers listed in relevant directories. They range from business schools offering MBA courses to small organisations specialising in short, single-subject courses, and selecting the right provider from this wide choice can be a daunting exercise.

Some large employers with their own training centres are able to meet most of their management training needs internally, although the organisation which is wholly self-reliant is extremely rare. Most organisations use external training providers for at least some of their requirements. The principal factors to bear in mind in selecting an external provider are:

- analysis of the organisation's needs
- systems of training provision
- identifying possible providers
- providers' character or style
- training costs.

Analysis of needs

The starting point must be an analysis of the organisation's training needs, and an assessment of which of these are to be met by external providers. The aim should be to produce a specification of what is required so that the search for a suitable source is clearly focused. There are two main dimensions to any management training needs analysis – the corporate requirements of the organisation, and the personal and career development needs of each individual manager. The first should be an element in the organisation's business plan. Individual needs can be identified through the appraisal process or assessment centres.

These various needs must then be categorised, as there are few, if any, training providers who operate so comprehensively as to be able to meet every identified training requirement. The categories are likely to include:

- management education, which can usefully be subdivided into the four levels of National Standards for Management of the Management Charter: supervisory, certificate (for first-level managers), diploma (for middle managers), and Masters (for senior managers with strategic responsibilities)
- skills and knowledge training in specific topics such as finance, quality management, IT skills, interviewing and very many other individual subjects. These need to be matched against those training providers who specialise in particular topics.
- personal and team development, or behavioural

training – another field in which there are numerous training specialists.

Systems of training provision

Various options then need to be considered as to how the required training should be provided. What may be a growing number of organisations commission a training provider to design and run training programmes in-house for top-level management education, eg company-based MBAs. Another expanding sector of the training market is the use of flexible or distance learning, such as the wide range of courses offered by the Open Business School. A growing number of universities, colleges and institutes have launched flexible training packages; the best include an element of personal coaching – by telephone and at weekend or summer schools.

Other options include the traditional but still useful part-time day release or sandwich courses. Short, off-the-job courses are useful for introductory management courses and for single-subject knowledge, skills and personal and team development training. For the latter, it is also necessary to decide whether to use outdoor training or the more conventional seminar-based format. The final option is full-time management education such as MBA courses at business schools, and the more comprehensive and lengthy management training programmes offered by centres such as Henley and Ashridge.

Identifying providers

The next step is to identify possibly suitable providers. There is no single source of fully comprehensive information. Directories will provide potted data on most training centres and this can be used to produce lists of organisations for more detailed examination. On a regional basis, TECs can supply details of approved training providers.

Events such as the IPD's annual conference and exhibition at Harrogate and HRD Work in London are good sources of information and provide useful opportunities to talk to training providers' representatives. Most professional institutes and many employers' associations can advise on training provision in their subject sectors. Many training sources advertise in the IPD's magazine, *People Management,* and will send material about their services and courses. Finally, recommendations may be obtained from personnel and development managers in other organisations.

From these sources it should be possible to draw up a shortlist of the providers who appear to meet the organisation's needs in terms of subject matter and the system of training. But facts about the content of programmes are not sufficient: an assessment of style and character is also important. Much of the success of any training activity lies with the chemistry between the tutors and the tutored, and even the most carefully prepared training material will miss its objectives if the managers under training feel uncomfortable with the style of presentation, or the culture or character of the training centre itself.

These factors can be assessed only by meeting potential tutors or visiting the training centres. Aspects of importance include:

- intellectual calibre. Managers from organisations with a large proportion of highly qualified staff involved in work demanding considerable intellectual effort may respond badly to tutors who deal with their subjects in an intellectually low key or popularised manner. Practical operational managers may similarly fail to gel with tutors who adopt an academic style. To avoid such problems, there should be some similarity of intellectual calibre as a basis for mutual recognition and respect.

- formality and structure. Training providers vary in the way they structure the learning process. Some adopt an informal and exploratory approach, requiring managers under training to contribute a great deal to the way a course develops. Others offer highly structured courses, delivered with a much greater degree of formality. Some provide large quantities of supportive documentation; others encourage managers to produce their own notes. Some make extensive use of case-studies; others place greater emphasis on teaching principles and theory. A view is needed as to which approaches best suit the organisation's managers.

- use of outside speakers. Training providers also vary in their use of outside speakers to supplement their own tutors. Some use none: others may rely almost wholly on speakers brought in. This needs to be examined closely, and the advantages of trainees hearing and being able to question eminent specialists or top managers, balanced against the possible disadvantages of a course which lacks coherence.

Three other practical issues need to be addressed. The

first is whether the training should be solely for the organisation's own managers, or whether there are greater benefits in open courses. The former permits a focus on the organisation's own plans and problems. Open courses give managers an opportunity to broaden their knowledge and extend their networks by meeting managers from other sectors. There are training centres that have become particularly widely used by overseas managers or by managers from one industry. The proportion of overseas MBA students at different business schools varies from 3 per cent to 90 per cent. Centres should be asked about this to avoid the risk of managers feeling out of place in courses dominated by another sector.

The second issue is whether the training should be residential. There is no doubt the intensity of training can be increased by using residential courses – even for two- or three-day events. Against this, there may be managers who, for domestic reasons, would have difficulty in attending such courses. If residential facilities are to be used they should be visited to ensure they match the organisation's preferred style.

The third issue is the extent to which in-house support will be needed to make the training a success. Courses which include project work will generally (and rightly) require commitment and assistance from senior management. Can this be guaranteed?

The costs
The cost of various options for management training is a significant factor, though preferably not an absolute determinant. The long-term value of effective training

should far exceed the difference in direct costs of good and less good training centres – not that the most expensive training is necessarily the best. It is as well, however, to be wary of training fees which are markedly out of line with general levels, although the decisive factor should always be quality. However, there is no point in paying more than is necessary, and it is on this point that the method of training, rather than its content, has a major impact. Residential courses are inevitably more expensive, and the quality (and cost) of residential facilities can also vary widely.

Distance learning may offer the least costly alternative for individuals, while the course delivered in-house by an external centre's staff will almost always be cheaper than sending staff to an open course teaching the same material. Open courses normally have fixed fees per student, ranging from as low as £150 to as high as £800 a day for short courses. Some trainers will provide similar courses run in-house for a flat fee of, say, £800 to £2,000 a day, regardless of the number attending. This fee will probably be negotiable, perhaps with a lower figure if the contract is to run a series of courses. Fees for full-time residential programmes run from around £5,000 to five-figures. For courses of high quality and of similar content and duration, large cost variations are rare. The choice here is very much a matter of finding the centre which best matches what the organisation is looking for, rather than selecting by price.

Further information

1 AP INFORMATION SERVICES. *The Personnel Manager's Yearbook.* AP Information Services, updated annually.

2 Mumford A. *Management Development: Strategies for action.* 3rd edn. London, Institute of Personnel and Development, 1997.

22 Training methods

The effectiveness of any training event is influenced by a variety of factors. Have the desired outcomes been defined? Is the level of training appropriate for the trainees? Do the trainees understand the purpose of the event and how it relates to their work? But however well these aspects have been addressed, the training will not be fully effective unless the appropriate method has been selected. Does the subject matter require any particular method or technique? For example, some aspects of safety training, such as the proper use of fire extinguishers, can be dealt with effectively only by practical demonstrations, whereas a topic such as appraisal interviewing can utilise several methods, such as role-plays, videos and personal coaching.

Is the training to be handled on an individual or group basis? The growth in the availability of self-learning packages, and in the concepts of mentoring, coaching and continuing personal development, has reduced the reliance on off-the-job training courses. What are the trainees' most effective learning styles? People differ in how they best learn. Some need to understand concepts before they try new skills; others learn best by plunging straight into a practical activity. One of the problems with group training is that the use of a standard training method will probably suit only some of the course attenders, although this can be overcome to some extent by including a mix of methods within the same course.

What outcome is required, in terms of knowledge, skills or attitudes? Helping trainees to improve their knowledge base requires different training methods from skills development or training designed primarily to change attitudes. What are the unit costs of the various alternative methods, and how do these relate to the targeted benefits? Group training, for example, may be less costly per head than individual training, but in some circumstances may be far less effective. The main types of training can now be considered with these questions in mind.

Group training methods

▪ lectures. Although still a common and low-cost training method, lecturers are one of the least effective. Research indicates that trainees retain only 20 per cent of the knowledge imparted in a lecture, while 10 minutes is about the outside limit for most people to maintain a high degree of attentiveness. Lectures can be improved with the use of OHPs, slides and video clips, which break the presentation into digestible portions. They are then best used for general scene-setting rather than for detailed knowledge inputs, or, provided the lecturer is sufficiently inspirational, to stimulate thinking about new ideas and so contribute to attitudinal change.

- group discussions. These have a low cost per head and can take several forms, though all carry the benefit of the active participation of the trainees. Typically, a large group will be split into small syndicates to discuss and play back their conclusions. In group tutorials, trainees are given a problem or project. They then prepare their individual responses and deliver these at the tutorial, where each person's views are probed by the tutor and the other trainees. This is a powerful method for testing how well new knowledge has been absorbed and for developing skills of argument and presentation. Another form of group discussion – brain-storming – is used primarily to stimulate creative thinking, though there is a risk of the discussion being dominated by a few highly articulate participants, and for the outcomes for a complex issue to be rather superficial.

- role-playing – such as the simulation of a board meeting to resolve a trading problem – requires the group to simulate real work behaviour, and is of use primarily to develop skills such as negotiation or team working. It can help to bridge the gap between theory and practice and is most effective with active and pragmatic learners. Theorists and introverts may be reluctant to join in, and may complain of the method's artificiality.

- films and videos can be used to impart new knowledge, illustrate new skills, demonstrate new processes and stimulate discussion. If well produced, they can hold trainees' attention far more effectively than a lecturer. However, there are two risks. First, the off-the-shelf production cannot reflect any one organisation's particular circumstances, so trainees may find it interesting but irrelevant. Second, some trainers use film or video simply as a break between more intensive learning activities, rather than as an integral part of the programme. But to gain full value they should be selected to meet a specific training objective – for example, to illustrate good and bad sales techniques.

- case studies can be selected to develop analytical and problem-solving skills, to provide a practical illustration of a principle or theory, or to develop team effectiveness. If the subject matter is related to the work of the organisation, this method can be more effective than role-playing in obtaining the active involvement of practically minded trainees.

- management games that simulate real-life situations can be effective in the practical application of concepts and procedures. They appeal to active and pragmatic learners, but may also engage the interest of more reflective or theoretical trainees, provided the purpose and principles are clearly explained.

- outdoor training. The primary purpose of most outdoor training is to develop team-working attitudes and skills, though for a group of mixed learning types there is a risk that activists and extroverts will gain more from the experience than others. To counter this tendency, the best outdoor programmes include classroom sessions in which concepts are discussed, and the lessons learnt in the outdoor environment are identified and analysed. Costs reflect the residential status of these courses, though they are usually cheaper than prestige residential management courses.

Individual training methods

- planned reading. Trainees who need to understand concepts or theories before committing themselves to more practical learning can benefit from programmes of planned reading. Some texts may also influence attitudes by sparking new thinking about organisational objectives or relationships. The method is almost useless for activists, while the very practical or pragmatic learner will probably respond only to short texts of the 'how to' variety.
- text-based open learning. Open or flexible learning programmes of the type developed by the Open Business School rely heavily on the study of textual material. Slanted towards (though not restricted to) the attainment of formal qualifications, most programmes demand considerable personal effort and are not effective unless the individual is strongly self-motivated. The emphasis is on the acquisition of knowledge, though many well-designed packages encourage or require the trainee to undertake project work to assist in skills development. Use of open learning can be helpfully linked to coaching and mentoring.
- IT-based open learning. There is a rapidly growing range of technology-based open learning packages on the market, and some trainers may have the

facility to produce in-house material. The methods include computer-based programmes, particularly for learning to use new software; interactive video (coupling the PC with a video player); interactive multimedia (using PC-based CD-Rom); and interactive CD, which combines a CD-i console with a television. This method's primary advantages are the requirement for the learner's full involvement, the wide range of subjects it can be used for, and the fact that trainees can pace their own learning. A subsidiary benefit is that whatever the topic, the process helps to develop computer literacy.

- coaching and mentoring. Coaching by a senior and mentoring by an experienced colleague are valuable training methods for the type of learner who benefits from support and personal encouragement. Coaching and mentoring can be used to reinforce more formal types of training, and is useful in helping employees put into practice what has been learnt on training courses or through private study.
- on-the-job training. Although 'sitting next to Nellie' has often been condemned as a flawed training method, systematic on-the-job training can be highly effective for some types of work. It is particularly suited to manual or other work which involves activities that are best learnt by a mixture of observation, explanation and practice. However, the tutor needs to have a good instructional skills and to follow a planned training sequence.

Further information

1 HONEY P. *and* MUMFORD A. *Manual of Learning Styles.* Maidenhead, McGraw-Hill, 1986.

2 REID M. *and* BARRINGTON H. *Training Interventions.* 5th edn. London, Institute of Personnel and Development, 1997.

3 *IPD Guide on Training Technology.* London, Institute of Personnel and Development, 1998.

23   Management games

It has long been recognised that the most effective selection tools are work simulation tests that replicate real tasks and require candidates to exercise skills that are relevant to the job. Many training and development professionals also believe that people learn best from planned and guided work experience – learning by doing.

Management games are a good way to combine both these ideals. Most are based around assessment centres and management development programmes, but there are also a significant number that simulate an impending situation in order to test proposed solutions, or to run through problems that may arise when the issue is tackled for real. 'Games' is a somewhat misleading description of what are generally intensive activities demanding effort and concentration. Line managers who assume that management games are lightweight may need to be reminded that game theory was devised by an economist and a mathematician (J. Neumann and O. Morgenstern: *Theory of Games and Economic Behaviour,*

Princeton University Press, 1947) and involves the creation of models that simulate complex operational situations.

Business or organisational simulation is a more accurate description of many of these games, although others use an activity unrelated to normal work, such as building a Lego tower to develop communication, negotiation and team skills. Many such activities also involve an element of competition, making them more akin to traditional sports. A management game should not be used simply because it provides an enjoyable break from more traditional developmental activities. From the trainer's point of view, games can be satisfying to run and the participants can find them stimulating. There is nothing wrong with a training activity that is fun, but the value of a management game is lost unless the right one is chosen to meet serious and clearly defined objectives.

In an assessment context, it is important to decide whether the primary goal of the game is to test current competence or to identify longer-term potential. If it is the former, participants need to be given tasks that highlight skills needed in their current work. But if the game is used to identity potential – as is more often the case – it should have a wider agenda and require participants to fill roles in which they may have had no experience but that are relevant to their future development. Games of this kind, often used to identify general management potential, may ask participants to take the roles of board members for functions other than their own, and to rotate the responsibility for leading the team as chief executive. The game may reflect the real commercial or organisational setting in which the participants would be working if they became senior managers.

For selection and training purposes, it is particularly important to be clear about the abilities that the management game should either test or help to develop. Some of these may be specific to the industrial sector or job function, such as the marketing of leisure services or pricing strategies for a manufacturing company. This is when off-the-shelf games should be treated with caution. If the subject of the game is insufficiently relevant, the participants may be unable or unwilling to translate the lessons into their own context.

In a training situation, management games are more often used to develop generic individual and team skills. Qualities such as the ability to be decisive under pressure, to analyse complex situations or to work constructively in a team are relevant to all organisational and commercial settings. These are the types of skills that well-designed management games can help to develop. There are some effective off-the-shelf games that can be used, and in this context the setting or content of a game may be much less important than its construction. Games with no obvious relevance to normal working tasks – such as building a Lego tower within tight rules and time limits – can focus powerfully on personal and interpersonal skills. Even where the activity is a direct business simulation, it may be useful for development purposes to set it in a commercial or organisational scenario that is different from that of the participants. A game that is closely related to the participants' real work may lead them to rely too much on their existing aptitudes and too little on developing skills to meet new demands. The key question is: do the tasks and roles of the game require them to exercise the skills identified in the training objectives?

At the same time, trainers should monitor the reaction of participants to any game that seems too far removed from their real work. If the exercise is seen as overly artificial, it may not be taken seriously. In other words, management games incur several risks. In order to obtain high scores or beat competing teams, participants may devote all their efforts into discovering how the trainer scores their efforts. They may find the exercise to be fun, but then fail to identify lessons that can be transferred into the workplace. An effective management game, therefore, helps participants to experience managerial or behavioural reality, even if the activity involved is removed from their everyday working life.

This raises the question about the use of competition. Many games simulate the performance of an organisation over a set period. For example, a game lasting six hours may simulate trading in a commercial environment over 12 months. Participants have to produce and revise their pricing and marketing plans throughout this period as various threats and opportunities are presented to them. A computer program continuously updates and analyses the results of their decisions and, at the end of the period, shows the resultant profit (or loss).

There are at least three ways to use a game of this kind, each with varying levels of competition. It can be run for a group of trainees in a single team, whose objective is to meet preset commercial targets. The only competitive element here stems from the activities of their simulated commercial adversaries. Alternatively, the participants could be required to work on their own, competing with each other as individual firms in the same marketplace. If there are enough participants, a third approach is to group them into several competing teams. In this scenario, it is also possible to allocate roles within the teams – finance, production, marketing, chief executive and so on, or to allow each team to decide which roles it needs, and to organise them itself. This approach can develop business know-how and team skills.

The potential benefits of building competition into a management game include the generation of a genuine feeling for the pressures inside a commercial environment. There is also a theory that the participants tend to take competitive business simulations more seriously, or at least put more energy and enthusiasm into them, because they are motivated by the chance of winning or losing against colleagues. However, while an emphasis on competition undoubtedly adds a sharper edge to games, this should not become the unstated priority over the other, possibly more important, learning objectives that they have been designed to achieve.

Business simulations may also be used to provide experience of situations that are likely to arise and to explore the possible solutions before the events actually happen. This use of management games is less common than the others, not least because it cannot be addressed with off-the-shelf training exercises. For this approach, it is vital that the simulation accurately mirrors an impending real-life situation. One recent example was a simulation of the processes involved in the reorganisation of local government structures, in which existing councils were disbanded and their services transferred to newly formed, all-purpose authorities. Before the transfers, managers of the councils that were being phased out met with their equivalents in the new authorities to work through a simulation of the whole process. This raised some important issues that had not previously been regarded as significant. It also provided the participants with experience in a variety of situations before they had to face them for real.

Further information

1. NILSON C. *Team Games for Trainers*. London, Institute of Personnel Management, 1993.

2. ADAIR J. *and* DESPRES D. *Handbook of Management Training Exercises*. London, BACIE/IPM, 1987.

24 Evaluating training

It is sometimes said that training is more an act of faith than a quantifiable contribution to the performance of organisations. While it is often hard to attribute specific financial improvements directly to the impact of training, this is not a reason for failing to conduct rigorous training evaluation. Indeed, the difficulties of showing direct links between at least some forms of training and their outcome in terms of benefit to the organisation emphasises the need for evaluation, even though this may be qualitative rather than quantitative. Training can be costly (though some effective forms of training are not), and trainers should be able to demonstrate the cost effectiveness of the training function, even when assessments are based mainly on the subjective, though informed, opinions of line managers.

Any training programme should be evaluated against the organisational needs it was intended to address: Was training the best way of meeting these needs? What specific outcomes were aimed for in terms of employees' performance? What training methods were used? Were these the most effective way of achieving the desired outcomes? Was the training conducted skilfully and cost effectively? Were the desired outcomes achieved?

Training needs

Simply considering whether targeted training outcomes have been achieved – the limit of some types of evaluation – is to risk missing a major preliminary point: the question of whether the right training needs were identified before the training began. In some cases there may even be a more fundamental question: was any analysis of training needs done at all? There have certainly been examples of organisations running the same training programmes for year after year without any real study of what needs are being addressed. Unintentionally, too, these needs may be biased towards the career development aspirations of the employee, with little attention to the needs of the business. The traditional public-sector concentration on training for professional qualifications may fall into this category.

So the first step in evaluation is to ask managers and trainers why they decided that a particular programme was required. Training plans should be an integral element of human resource planning, which in turn should be firmly rooted within the organisation's business plans. Is training the right answer? It is one thing to identify an organisational need – for greater attention, say, to quality. It is another matter to decide whether this need is best addressed by a formal training programme. Training is not always the best way of correcting shortcomings in organisational performance.

It might be better to make changes to work systems,

or to the way jobs are structured, or to recruitment and selection methods. Some managers tend to see formal training as the answer to almost every problem, and some trainers reinforce this attitude by never questioning requests by managers for training assistance. The generalist personnel manager (and the wise trainer) will always explore a range of possible solutions before suggesting an expensive training programme.

Outcomes

No training should be undertaken without a clear view of its desired outcomes. If a manager or trainer cannot specify in advance what the training is designed to achieve, it is impossible to justify its expense or evaluate its impact. Of course, some hit-or-miss training may, by accident, achieve worthwhile results, but this is no way for a professional function to acquire credibility.

Ultimately, most targeted outcomes can be expressed in terms of changes that the training is designed to achieve in employees' work behaviour and performance. It is often helpful to evaluate this in stages, particularly if improvements in performance may be influenced by action parallel to training, such as the redesign of work systems or the use of new equipment.

The first stage in setting training objectives may therefore be to target some very specific outcomes, such as the extent to which trainees understand and remember the knowledge they have acquired immediately after their course. For longer-term assessment, outcomes can relate to how well trainees apply this knowledge at work. Skills or competency-based outcomes can be defined in terms of measurable quality or quantity targets, possibly within a time limit. For example, an outcome for production workers might be defined as: 'Achieve the average performance rating for experienced operators, with less than 1 per cent rejects, within six months of recruitment'.

Less specific outcomes may have to be set for broader-based training, particularly for managers, eg 'to demonstrate significant improvements in the quality of team leadership, as assessed within the formal appraisal process'. The important point is to define outcomes in ways that aid the eventual assessment of results. Targets such as 'improve managerial standards' are too vague.

Training methods

The evaluation should include an assessment of whether the training methods used were the most suitable and cost effective. Similar outcomes may be achieved by a variety of training techniques, and less costly alternatives to formal, off-the-job courses are too often overlooked. The range of methods has grown considerably in recent years, with an increasing emphasis on self-learning and distance techniques and the use of computerised packages and interactive video. Trainers should be able to show they have assessed alternative training methods and selected the most cost effective.

Assessing cost effectiveness can be aided by obtaining relevant benchmarking data, not only about financial indicators (such as daily per capita training costs) but also in identifying examples of best practice by other organisations for the same or similar types of training.

Conduct of training

The effectiveness of a training programme may be significantly influenced by the skill of the trainer in whatever techniques are used. The benefit of accurate needs analysis, clear definition of outcomes and selection of appropriate techniques can be lost if the trainer lacks competence in managing the training and learning process. This is a particular risk when using difficult techniques such as assertiveness training or when an enthusiastic but inexperienced trainer experiments with outdoor training. Part of the evaluation should be an assessment of the trainer's competence in handling the type of training adopted.

Achievement

The core of the evaluation process is the assessment of changes in the trainees' knowledge, conduct, attitude and work performance, relative to the targeted outcomes. There are a number of ways this can be tested.

Face validity can be examined through evaluation questionnaires for the trainees, asking their views of the effect and value of training. These may be issued as soon as training is completed and then repeated several months later. Immediate responses need to be treated with great caution, as the first reaction to training may be very superficial – and sometimes euphoric.

Many programmes designed to improve trainees' knowledge and understanding of specific topics (eg health and safety rules or financial procedures) lend themselves to a post-training test. Participants answer forced-choice questions, either on paper or at a computer terminal. Some software packages provide a framework into which organisations can insert their own test questions, and they also provide an analysis facility, producing management data about trainees' test performance.

Tests can go beyond simply checking gains in knowledge. They can pose questions about work situations and ask the trainees to select a response. For example:

> You discover a small fire in the stockroom. What is the first thing you would do: a) Telephone for help b) Try to put the fire out c) Sound the fire alarm?

The shortcoming with such questions is that, while the trainee may give the right answer in the test, this does not guarantee the right behaviour in a real work situation. On the other hand, the test itself can be built into the learning process, by feeding back results to each trainee and providing material for follow-up coaching and revision.

For some types of training it is possible to measure trainees' performance before and after training. This applies to many manual and sales jobs. Factors such as productivity, error or complaint rates, sales volumes, time taken to complete standard work transactions, unit costs and the like can all be assessed. Training evaluators need to check the availability of management information of this kind.

Appraisals are a rich source of information about changes in performance, provided the factors examined in the appraisal process can be related to training objectives. This provides the most direct form of evaluation when the appraisal itself is used to identify training needs, set training and development goals and discuss outcomes. When the connection between appraisal and training course objectives is not so clear cut, evaluation may need to include interviews with managers, or for them to complete questionnaires about aspects of ex-trainees' performance which are specific to the training programme.

The benefits of thorough evaluation extend beyond a simple assessment of the cost effectiveness of the training itself. Evaluation can indicate areas for improvement in training objectives or delivery and, by involving managers in the evaluation process, their interest and commitment to training can be enhanced. But if one point needs emphasis, it is that effective evaluation depends on the clear definition of targeted training outcomes.

Further Information

1 BRAMLEY P. *Evaluating Training.* London, Institute of Personnel and Development, 1996.
2 BOYDELL T. *and* LEARY M. *Identifying Training Needs.* London, Institute of Personnel and Development, 1996.

25   Preparation for retirement

Employers with a sense of responsibility for the well-being of their staff recognise that, for some, the change from full-time employment to retirement can be a traumatic and disorienting experience. The provision of various forms of pre-retirement preparation, therefore, now forms an important element within their set of personnel practices.

The case for providing pre-retirement assistance, however, goes beyond this welfare-focused view. Many employers believe that retirement can to some extent be managed as a way of introducing more flexibility into staff resourcing. Voluntary early retirement can release promotion blockages and help prevent enforced redundancies.

The employment of retired staff on occasional or project work, perhaps on a consultancy basis, may also enable organisations to cope better with fluctuating workloads. Additionally, the reputation of an organisation as a caring employer, and hence its ability to recruit, retain and motivate employees, is enhanced by its being seen to recognise the need for assistance that many employees have in the transition to retirement.

Pre-retirement preparation is sometimes thought of simply in terms of a training course which all impending retirees are invited to attend shortly before their last day at work. While this is a great deal better than nothing, more benefit can be obtained by taking a longer-term and broader view, in which a short pre-retirement course is only one element.

Personnel practitioners putting together a comprehensive pre-retirement policy will need to consider what long-term preparation for retirement will be available, what the company's policy on retirement ages will be, what provision will be made for job changes before retirement, and what individual counselling will be available.

They will also need to look at pre-retirement courses, in terms of participants, duration and content, and location and cost, at post-retirement measures, and at the degree of assistance that will be required from outside the company.

Long-term preparation

For some aspects of retirement, preparation needs to begin many years before the event. One of the most serious problems is that of the employee who retires on an inadequate pension due to insufficient attention during earlier stages of employment. This has become an increasingly important factor in retirement planning since the abolition of compulsory membership of occupational pension schemes, and with the diminishing extent of lifetime service with one employer.

Young employees may make short-term decisions and decide not to join a company scheme, or to take out a personal pension plan. This indicates a need for advice on pension costs, options and benefits at a very early stage in an employee's career.

It is helpful to begin more specific pre-retirement programmes as long as 10 years before retirement, with a short course for staff around age 50 to 55 to focus attention on the value of personal retirement planning. Individual counselling may be offered at least a year before retirement.

Retirement age

The programming and content of pre-retirement preparation will be influenced by an organisation's policy regarding retirement age. With fixed retirement ages, retirement is seen by staff as a compulsory and abrupt cut-off point, although for employers it makes the timing of pre-retirement courses and estimates of the numbers of staff involved and the costs very predictable.

There may, however, be some negative attitudes to address in retirement counselling with a fixed-age policy, both from those who would have preferred to retire earlier and others who wish to continue at work. Many organisations are introducing flexibility into retirement, with staff able to choose a retirement date between, say, 50 and 60. In this case, early information about the effect on pensions of different retirement options becomes a high priority.

Job changes

There are jobs at all levels in which the physical or mental demands may place undue pressure on some older employees. This is not a matter for generalised assumptions or practices: some staff in older age groups remain fully capable of meeting the most arduous job requirements and would be deeply offended by any action which implied otherwise.

On an individual basis, however, if it is evident (and agreed by the employee concerned) that the pressures of work are becoming too great, caring employers will look for ways of easing this situation. This may involve a transfer to a less pressurised job, the provision of additional assistance, a change in job design, or perhaps a transition from full-time to part-time working during the last year of employment.

Individual counselling

This last point illustrates that employees' attitudes towards retirement, the extent to which they need advice, and which issues that advice should deal with, may vary considerably from one person to another. Ideally, each impending retiree should have the opportunity of a confidential counselling discussion, so that any matters of personal concern can be addressed.

Some employees will have made their own retirement preparation and need no assistance at all. It would be a mistake to treat all retirees as though they invariably faced major problems.

Courses

The most common form of assistance is pre-retirement courses. There are two approaches to arranging attendance. Some practitioners argue that as retirement is an experience common to all employees, course attendance is best organised on a status-free basis, mixing employees from every type and level of job.

Others have found it better to group staff from broadly similar jobs. Financial planning for a manager retiring on a £25,000 pension is very different from the problems of, and therefore the advice given to, a manual worker who may be relying primarily on state benefits.

It is a mistake, however, to assume that managerial staff would not benefit from course attendance. Managers who have gained considerable satisfaction from the interesting jobs, which have dominated their lives, may feel a greater loss of purpose when they retire than many manual or office workers (who often see retirement as a welcome escape from boring work).

The value of a course can be enhanced by involving employees' partners. Retirement often means couples have to establish new patterns of relationships at home, and the involvement of both partners in discussion and advice about retirement is generally to be encouraged.

Most pre-retirement courses vary between six and 30 hours in length, though the sessions may be spread across several days or even weeks, as an alternative to full-time day or weekend courses. Because the subject matter is so varied, and because much of the input has to be knowledge-based, there is much to be said for a series of one or two-hour sessions over a period of several weeks.

A comprehensive course which attempts to deal with all the important aspects of retirement would normally include:

- pensions, occupational and State
- other social security benefits

- personal taxation
- investment (eg of retirement lump sums)
- health and fitness
- leisure activities and opportunities
- personal relationships
- home activities and house maintenance.

There are three main options as to where a pre-retirement course can be held. They can take place in-house, using an organisation's training centre or conference rooms, or away from work, perhaps at a hotel. (This is particularly appropriate if the aim is to involve employees and spouses in an intensive residential weekend event.) The final option is a location provided by an external agency such as a college or the premises of a specialist consultancy, if the organisation itself has not the expertise, time or facilities to run an adequate course in-house.

The choice will be influenced partly by the style of the course and partly by cost considerations. A residential weekend at a high-standard hotel is the most expensive option, and a series of one-hour sessions in-house the least costly, with the cost per head varying from several hundred pounds to a purely nominal figure in the case of modest in-house events.

Post-retirement

Caring employers do not abandon contact with employees once they become pensioners. Many retired people appreciate their organisation keeping in touch through newsletters and occasional social events, while others may need more direct and personal advice on a counselling basis when problems arise. Some organisations offer welfare visits to their retired employees, or provide a telephone help-line.

For some retired staff, it may be helpful both to the organisation and the employee to provide occasional work, such as covering for sickness or holiday absences, or undertaking specific projects. Retired professional or executive staff who wish to remain active but for whom additional earnings are not a priority may also be helped by putting them in touch with the charity Reach, which can find them part-time, expenses-only work with charitable organisations.

External help

It is often difficult for busy personnel generalists to find the time or acquire the specialist expertise needed to provide adequate pre-retirement preparation. Information and advice on topics such as lump sum investments, tax and social security benefits need to be totally accurate and impartial, and few personnel managers would claim to be experts in these fields. There are also statutory regulations which limit the giving of financial advice to qualified specialists.

In consequence, external assistance is often desirable. This can be arranged in a number of ways. For example, individual experts, such as a bank manager, a health and fitness specialist and an independent investment adviser, can be invited to contribute sessions to in-house courses.

Alternatively, staff can be booked on to standard pre-retirement courses run by organisations such as local colleges, the Workers Educational Association or specialist consultancies.

More comprehensive forms of assistance can be

arranged through the Pre-Retirement Association (PRA), a national authority on mid-life and retirement planning which is part-funded by government. The PRA offers training for personnel managers who wish to qualify as retirement counsellors, as well as general consultancy and training services covering every aspect of retirement.

Further Information

1 WALKER, J. *Preparing for Retirement: The employer's guide.* London, Age Concern, 1992.

2 HUGHES, K. *Retirement Counselling.* Maidenhead, McGraw-Hill, 1992.

3 Pre-Retirement Association: 26 Frederick Sanger Road, Surrey Research Park, Surrey, GU2 5YD (01483 301170).

4 Reach: 27 Bankside, London SE1 9ET (0171 928 0452).